FIGURE THAT SHIFT OUT: AN INVITATION TO RELAX INTO YOUR BRILLIANCE

Printed in the United States of America

Brandi, Ashlynn, Madi, and Brae:
You teach me. Thank you. Thank you for supporting
all it has taken to get this message out.

Bret, so this was harder than I thought.
Thanks for digging deep.

Adam, you brought the unblocking and
the reminder that it was gonna be ok.

Tim, you kept reminding me of the diamonds.
I still want to be a pink sparkly one.

Amanda, thank you for the precision and accuracy.

The test of a first-rate intelligence is the ability to hold two opposed ideas in the mind at the same time, and still retain the ability to function.

F. SCOTT FITZGERALD

INTRODUCTION

While I type this my next coaching meeting is in line getting her coffee. I wish you could be here. The conversations, the formative exercises, and the vulnerable processing form this elixir that gives me this feeling of I-can't-believe-I-get-to-help-people-from-my-pain.

What you're about to read started as an email course. Those in the coaching program would get an email, an audio to listen to and exercises to complete. The first four chapters will take you deep into the problem. Then you'll be ready for the next four chapters that will empower you with solutions. The last four chapters will help you fine-tune the results. It's your leadership pathway. You need a unique and customized solution. This book is your guide to help you figure that out.

I'm not a leadership coach that tells you what to do. I want to help you learn to figure out who you are and how to overflow your brilliant self to the world around you.

I've attempted to distill down the most critical information with the insights from almost 150,000 words I've written about identity and 1000's of hours of conversations. If you want to hear the audios that went with the email course you can find a link to the podcast at chrismcalister.com. Go to the beginning 12 episodes that correspond with each chapter.

I'm so glad you're here.

TABLE OF CONTENTS

CHAPTER ONE
REFRAME EVERYTHING

The privilege of a lifetime is
to become who you truly are.
CARL JUNG

I can't imagine going to the grocery store before cell phones. If I don't have specific items on the list, I feel overwhelmed. During one visit to the grocery store, one item on the list my wife made for me simply read: "pineapples." That single word triggered a dilemma: What kind of pineapples? Did she want a real pineapple that you have to cut? Maybe she meant the already-cut pineapple in the little plastic container or dried pineapple in a bag. Did she mean canned pineapple, canned pineapple chunks, canned pineapple tidbits, or canned pineapple slices? Did she want heavy syrup or 100% juice? At this point, I felt so overwhelmed that all I wanted was pineapples soaked in vodka.

At that moment, I understood the reason I was frustrated and irritated by that single word—I didn't want to mess up. Most of us don't realize there's an ugly, false narrative pulsating through our life, our leadership, and our work. We buy into that narrative and it is that false narrative keeps us from being able to bring the full expression of who we are to our life and leadership. Most of us are not secure in our uniqueness. We do not know how to organize our day or week around our energy, our passion, and our interest. We're not able to process what's happening to us and make clear decisions because we're so blinded by this narrative.

Learn to order your internal world so you can lead your external world. Your brain is so hungry for a narrative that it will create a false one. When we learn to recognize false narratives, we can experience freedom from the frustration. I'm going to teach you a sequence that will become a foundation for future growth.

Have you driven a manual transmission or stick-shift car? Most people have had some experience driving one. Even if you haven't, you've probably ridden in a car with a manual transmission or have seen a car stuck at a stop sign when the driver couldn't shift into first gear and the car shut down.

I was 16 years old taking my white Honda Civic out for my first Friday night. I was so excited about my new freedom. My friend, Jerry, was with me and we were going to hang out with friends. The first stoplight I came to after leaving my house was on a hill. This was a crisis. The light turned green and I tried to shift into first gear, but I couldn't get it to work. The car rattled and shut down. The light changed back to red and we had not moved. Drivers in the cars behind us were becoming impatient.

I was freaking out. My teenage sweat glands weren't made for this pressure. We sat motionless while the light cycled from red back to green. Again. Rattle. Shut down. When the light was about to turn green for the third time Jerry said, "I'm going to show you a trick." He jerked up the emergency brake and said, "Go ahead and shift into first. Lightly press the gas." The light turned green and Jerry dropped the emergency brake. My car screeched out of the intersection and I quickly regained control. A minute later we were on the highway, riding free.

I want to explain to you what blocks up your leadership. It keeps you from making great decisions; it keeps you from being able to move in and out of the roles you fill in a healthy way; it's how you get in your own way or become your own worst enemy: You're trying to force your life into second gear by completely skipping first gear.

If you're driving a stick shift, you can shift straight into second gear on a flat surface. The same is true in life. You can start out on the smooth stretches of life going straight into second gear. It works. Unfortunately, when you hit the hills of life – the hard times and the complex situations – you may have a lot of success around you, but on the inside you know something is off. Or maybe you don't have those indicators of success around you and you feel discouraged when all the hard work you've put into a relationship or job isn't enough.

Downshifting isn't just important when we're driving uphill. The highest performing drivers in the world use downshifting all the time. They downshift to accelerate momentum in sharp turns and to navigate in and out of heavy traffic. They also downshift to save wear and tear on their brakes. Shifting to a lower gear is the best option for both performing through the hills of life, but also for winning an ultra competitive race.

More intensity isn't going to fix your problem. More intensity won't get you off the hill. More intensity won't allow you to capitalize on the momentum of the turn. I could have tried to ram the car into second gear with as much intensity as I wanted when I was on that hill, and it wouldn't have worked. I had to learn the finesse of shifting into first gear on the hill. I needed clarity. That's the same thing you need. Think about your life in three areas, like gears of a car. First gear is your identity; who you are. Second gear is your mission, your work; it's what you do and the roles you fulfill. Third gear is your community; the relationships in your life.

Identity, Mission, Community

Our life consists of three pieces: Identity, mission, community. First, second, and third gear. An easy way to spot yourself trying to shift straight into second gear is when you hear yourself asking, "Am I contributing and do people like me?" These are the driving questions cultivated by thousands of years of evolutionary biology. You've been conditioned to believe if you don't contribute or if you mess up then you won't get a share of the wooly mammoth meat. If they don't like you or you're annoying, then you'll get kicked out the cave and will die. (I had a college roommate who would borrow toiletries like my deodorant and my toothbrush without asking. There were many mornings when I wanted to shout "Get out of my cave!") Freedom is living from a secure identity apart from what you do and your relationships.

We have conflated being and doing, and now we need to separate them to downshift. We need to learn to process life, to reframe it, so that when bad things happen to us we're not crushed, and when good things happen to us a euphoric high doesn't blind us to what led to those good things. We want to be able to repeat the actions that created the good results. Paradoxically, when we learn to reframe, we accelerate our life by downshifting into first gear. We unblock a higher level of performance. We find freedom from insecurity when we root ourselves in a secure identity. We learn to relax our way into who we are. We find flow.

The concept of identity can seem nebulous, but I want to make it feel very concrete to you. The greatest insights we have had psychologically over the last few hundred years have been related to understanding this concept of identity. Freud had a negative bent—you're trying to get back to something you had or make up for something you didn't get. Others, like Carl Jung, claimed that the search for identity is actually positive. Erikson claimed that identity developed in stages and laid out the stages of development in adolescence. Yet another severe misunderstanding continued: the identity of an adult is fixed. Researchers like Robert Kegan proved what you're already familiar with every time your family gets together: Adults aren't static. They're going through processes and changes, too.

There's a pattern in our life where we fail to cooperate with how our lives change. We jump into life, and we make naïve decisions that are based on hype and bravado. Eventually we start to question things. The hills of life come. A lot of us stuff those questions down. Then things usually start to crack apart as if life is trying to seize our attention. Instead of taking time to pay attention to the key questions, we usually try some distracting intervention. A new relationship, a new purchase, or an off-the-wall decision hides the fact we're grasping at straws to feel alive.

We can cooperate with our how our lives change rather than fight against it. Individuals that have left a lasting and positive impact on history knew how to cooperate with it. They lived out of a secure identity. They pursued their mission single-mindedly. They built community around that mission.

Introspection Is Necessary

Whether you know it or not, the great challenge of your life is to figure out who you are. You're on a search for identity. What we're going to go through as we walk through the process in this book is introspective. I'm going to teach you how to recognize the power of the smallest moments of your life, even if that introspection might feel awkward. For many, a honed introspection is not a muscle you're used to using.

I live in the Midwest and it's pretty cold here in the winter. I've grown to love running but last winter I fell off the wagon. It was so cold, as in below-freaking-zero-cold, that I wasn't running very much. In February, I decided to begin running regularly again. There's a six-mile loop I was confident I could do. Two miles into my first run of the year my teardrop muscles, the vastus medialis muscles above my knees, started to cramp from not being used. The pain wasn't a light twinge. My muscles cramp was so intense that I had to stop on the side of the road, bend down, and try to stretch the muscles by resting on my knees. It definitely wasn't the proudest moment in my athletic career. When the excruciating pain continued to throb, I knew I couldn't complete the loop. My first thought was I could try to walk back, but the seizing muscles made that impossible. I had to hobble-run the entire two miles back to my house. I was in so much pain the next day that I had to cancel speaking engagements.

Throughout the next chapters, I will be asking you to engage exercises that require you to use your introspection. Some of your mental muscles may feel like cramping because this introspection is going to open you up to think about who you are (identity), what you do (mission), and who you relate to (community). Most people don't realize that the false narrative we have bought into—the story we're living out that's driving us from a core fear—can be understood if we search within.

Every day we are trying to get something from others to meet the insecure need of our identity. Every day we go about our doing trying to get something for our identity. Every day we're hiding who we are, convinced that we're not whole apart from what we do and our relationships.

I have 15 years of experience leading non-profits and starting businesses. I have had ventures succeed and I have had ventures fail. In one particular season I applied all my energy trying to see a venture turn around, but nothing changed. It was grueling. It was painful. I was trying to figure out how to buy groceries and pay for medicine when the kids became sick. I clearly remember the moment I opened the pantry to fix myself a bowl of Cheerios and stopped myself. If I had eaten those Cheerios, my kids would not have had breakfast the next day. My wife sold her engagement ring so we could buy Christmas presents for our children. I went from being a part of a multi-million dollar company, to all of that going away and being six zeroes in debt. As if that wasn't enough pressure, the income I was used to making had gone down by 80 percent. I can blame being bald on that, right?

As a result of all of that chaos, our family came home one beautiful summer evening to find an eviction notice taped to our door. I felt like someone had ripped out my guts. The next day I remember sitting on the deck feeling like a failure. I felt like I was scraping the bottom of my soul and I could not stir up anything to grab ahold of. It was there that I stumbled into a technique that opened me up to the power of living from a secure identity.

I asked myself a few questions. Am I worth more as a human being if we stay in our house? Am I worth less as a human being if we have to leave our house? I pictured us leaving. I pictured us staying. I felt the failure of the eviction and noticed the emotions. I mentally pushed myself to imagine the worst and best scenario. Mentally, I contrasted the negative and positive to see myself as whole and secure in my identity regardless of whether or not we stayed or went. I thought, "If we have to move, if we have to leave this house next week and have to move into a moldy apartment, I'm not defined by this." This isn't about the hype of visualization that says if you can picture something then it will happen. This is about transcending your circumstances.

We all want to be resilient. We all want to find our brilliance. We all want to flow. We don't want to be hardened by our battles, we want to grow smarter through them. We want to become more whole through them and we want to develop the skills so we don't get shut down. We want to persevere in our mission. We want to persevere in the relationships that we have made and commitments to those we love.

How are we going to be resilient? We have to learn to notice our form. We pay attention to how we engage life. We become aware of how we frame what is happening to us. Stress, whether real or perceived, shows us the breakdown in our form or internal posture. Stress exposes the false narrative. After the stress from our hills, or the mental stress from our imagined hills, we learn to rebuild our form. We learn to reframe. We learn to separate who we are from what we do. We learn we are secure regardless of how others treat us. We are not defined by what happens in our mission. We are not defined by our relationships or what others think of us.

While I was sitting on the deck, I resolved: "I am separate from the events that are happening to me. I'm not defined by them. I am more than this leader who feels like he's failing, this husband who feels like he's failing, and this father who feels like he's failing."

Once, during that season of struggle, my kids wanted to ride a Ferris wheel at a nearby carnival but I couldn't afford the ticket. The ticket was only five dollars. I went to the pawn shop to sell a digital picture frame that someone had given us for Christmas so I could buy a ride for all three of my daughters. I could only get 10 dollars for the picture frame. When you face that kind of humiliation, you have to learn who you are. On those hills of life you have to shift into first gear, and if you don't, you're stuck. How many people do you know who are shut down and stuck?

I want you to know this: You are not defined by what you have done. You are not defined by your mistakes. You are not defined by your losses or even your wins. Learn your identity is separate from your mission and your community. You have the ability to choose what you are defined by. You're empowered in this. There is no greater choice.

I know there are some people who are trying to escape the modern angst of living by believing the self is an illusion. The answer to this search for identity is not to ignore it and disregard the self as real. The answer is to understand there is something happening here and you need to learn to pay attention so you can start to figure out who you are. It takes time. It takes energy. It takes introspection but when you learn to downshift to your identity, everything else can and will change.

Check Your Filter

When my wife and I first married, I didn't know anything about home repairs. I hate fixing stuff. We moved into an apartment and one day our air shut down. I asked the landlord to have someone check our air. He responded, "Have you checked the filter?" The filter? I asked, "What is the filter you speak of?" He said, "That's your problem." He told me where the filter was. I unscrewed the panel and there was the most disgusting, filthy and gunked-up filter you could imagine. Since then, I've set it as a task reminder to replace it every month.

I had to get a new filter. You may need your filter cleaned. There's probably already some healthy processing, but for most, you need a completely new filter. You have defined who you are by what you do. You have defined who you are by your relationships. First gear first. Do you want to accelerate your life? Reframe everything and downshift into first gear. This is how you're going to learn to order your internal world.

I'm going to tell you stories that help you learn how to reframe what's happening in the smallest of moments. Why? So you can learn to live from a secure identity. A secure identity overflows to a clear mission and builds a healthy community. That's a life that isn't stuck. That's flow. Flow increases its presence in our life when fear decreases its presence. And shopping doesn't require pineapples soaked in vodka.

Exercises To Complete:

1. Who are you?

2. What do you do? What happens if you win? If you lose? Go back to the part about the eviction. Find a circumstance in your life where things are going great or bad and contrast the picture. Downshift by considering the security of your identity whether circumstances are exhilarating or disappointing.

3. What about the relationships you have in your life? In what way are you building who you are around their love and acceptance of you, their celebration of you, their lack of appreciation for you, or their lack of celebration for you?

4. What are the roles you fulfill? What happens in those roles if you fulfill them the way you expect of yourself? Do you think that makes your identity more secure? More whole? Are you falsely building and evaluating who you are around the highs and lows of mission or community?

CHAPTER TWO

NO MORE PROVING & HIDING

The essence of leadership is being aware of your fear.
SETH GODIN

To make sense of your own story as a leader, you need to pay attention to what's happening on the inside. Until you learn to order your internal world, you will fail in ordering your external world. Reframing your identity, mission, and community will help you downshift into your first, most fundamental gear. Living your life out of a secure identity produces flow. Fear blocks flow.

The Fear Narrative

A few years ago my friends signed me up for an obstacle course race. Ten whole miles! A busy season in my life left me sedentary and out of shape. I needed to start training again, but the only time my schedule permitted me to run was at night. I'm typically wiped out by the end of the day. I desperately needed extra motivation. It came in the form of an app that synced my exercise to a mission in which I had to flee from zombies. The app interrupted my music with a narrative about the mission and how close the zombies were to pouncing on me. You hear the zombies getting closer to you or farther away at different points in the app. At the same time I was immersed in this training regimen, I was teaching a few college courses during the day and my students were raving about a TV show, The Walking Dead. Their weekly conversations about the show convinced me to watch it. Between the show and the app, my life was inundated with zombies, almost to the point I believed I saw real zombies. One evening while I was at the climax of my running mission app, a man walked out between two houses. I had to look at him and tell myself, "That's not a zombie, it's a human being." But he was coming towards me quickly, and my brain started to wonder, *What if?* This zombie narrative from the show and my running app was getting deep into my psyche.

Late one night, I was working at our kitchen table after everyone else had gone to sleep. The house was quiet and my running playlist was on in the background. Then the song came on where the zombies in the app usually start chasing me. As I was sitting there typing and the song came on, I reflexively turned and looked over my shoulder. I was in a safe, warm house with the doors locked. It wasn't real, but it *felt* real.

I might joke about seeing "walkers" in the corn field near my house but when real fears are driving you, it hurts. Everything hinges on understanding this: You can't reframe everything in your life until you gain awareness of the fear narrative that is driving your actions. It is the fear narrative that keeps you from being fully engaged in your life and leadership. Your work isn't the true reflection of who you are and your relationships aren't the free expression of you because fear blocks the truth. When you understand your fear you unblock everything. Multiple leaders, business voices, and sages throughout time have been saying this. Learn how you have been triggered to be afraid. I built a trigger of fear with a running app without even trying to do it. Experiences build our triggers. Throughout your life, some big things have happened and lots of small things have happened, and all of them have reinforced a response of fear.

Proving And Hiding

The way to recognize a fear response is when you feel yourself trying to hide or trying to prove. We prove and hide every day without being aware of this coping mechanism. As you learn to recognize this in your life, you're going to learn how to cooperate with a process of change. Long before you prove and hide to others you will prove and hide to yourself. Learning to quickly recognize when you are proving or hiding opens up your ability to reframe and re-center. As you learn to process your life along the lines of identity, you're cooperating with how you grow and the beginning of growth is to be aware of your fear rather than to hype yourself past it. Right now, there are people around you who are trying to prove something to you. They're trying to prove something in the board room. They're trying to prove something at home. People say pride is the problem. Pride isn't the problem. Fear is. Have you ever met a secure narcissist? I haven't. They're trying to prove something because they don't believe it's true. Taking initiative and staying active in leadership and relationships doesn't have to be powering up. It all depends on whether the actions and behavior are from the overflow of a secure or an insecure identity.

Other people are hiding. They're diminishing who they are. They're diminishing the contribution they could make to that project at work. They're diminishing the fullness of their presence in that relationship. We all prove and hide in some way every day.

I'll walk you through nine different fears to help you get clarity on who you are and what fear is driving your life right now.

Fear Of Not Being Needed

"If I'm not needed, then I'm not loved." There are people right now who are making horrible relationship decisions. They're making awful business and leadership decisions. Leaders with this fear don't develop a team of peers. They keep systems in place to make sure they are needed. They're trying to keep people connected to them because they think if others don't need them then they won't fit in.

If you believe this fear about yourself, you will prove to people how they need you. This will cause you to self-sabotage. You will push them away because of your insecurity. That insecurity is going to push away the very advancement you want at work or the very relationship you want to flourish.

When this fear is driving you and a relationship ends or a season of being needed stops then you will feel lost. The painful moment can be an opportunity for a wake up call to learn who you are. You do not have to say yes to every request for help.

Fear Of Not Being Cared For

"If I don't take care of myself, no one else will." This is when you feel like it's all on your shoulders. There's no place where you can let go and rest and know you are taken care of. If this is the fear that dominates your horizon, if this is how you are approaching life, then you are never going to come to a place where you feel joy. You feel abandoned and alone. You can recognize this fear is at work when you believe your needs are a problem. If you feel everybody around you is selfish, it might be that you resent the fact they are taking care of themselves while you play the part of the martyr. You need a big permission slip that says, "Take care of yourself."

Again, there is a reason this fear is there. Our lives have triggered our brains to believe these fears. We'll talk some about the brain later, but for now, remember these fears are false even though they feel real. Whatever you have been through in your mission or your community that has imprinted these fears is not true about who you are.

In order to cooperate with the process of how our lives change, we need to find that abundant security within. You'll still have to go out, work, and make things happen. You can't kick your feet up and say, "I'm going to be taken care of, I don't have to apply myself." But when you know your identity is taken care of internally, then externally you can apply all the energy you need to your mission and your community. All the love that you need—all the acceptance, all the celebration—is already inside you. Later, I'll teach you how to tap into that flow, but for now we're identifying the fears.

Fear Of Not Belonging

"I don't belong anywhere." If this is your fear, you are constantly looking for a place to call home. You hope that finally, this will be the relationship where you can be fully known for who you are. Or finally, this job or role will be your tribe. People that are driven by this fear want belonging because they aren't at peace within. They are trying to get peace by focusing on belonging so they can forget their problems. By obsessively trying to fit in, they distract themselves by kicking their problems further down the road. They don't have the energy to solve their problems because they have bought into a lie that peace is the absence of problems.

Peace isn't the absence of problems. It's having the energy required to address and solve what is in front of you. People who are always wondering if they belong can't have peace. They are so distracted by trying to fit in that they are unable to focus on their problems.

This is the person who is needy at work, trying to get constant assurance that they're seen and known for who they are. They prove they belong by referencing what they have been doing with others or they hide in the corner afraid to engage and be further left out. When we fear that we don't belong anywhere, we have bought into the narrative that, in our identity, we don't have a home.

Fear Of Inadequacy

"I don't have what it takes." You're fixing the car with Dad and he pushes you out of the way and says, "That's easy. I'll do it." Children are great recorders but terrible interpreters, and they interpret their experiences into a false narrative of not being enough. In this fear, your interpretation is to never do something you can't do flawlessly. As a result, you will only focus your energy into the spaces you know you can be exceptional. You hyper-specialize in one area, but in other areas of life you're afraid of failure so you don't engage. Maybe you kill it at work, but you're floundering at home. What do you need? You need an internal, secure identity full of patience. You can take the successful work skills you have developed and use those skills and techniques to be awesome relationally, too.

The fear that you will be inadequate, you don't have what it takes, and that you're not enough is hanging around your neck and holding you back.

Fear Of Poor Performance

"I can't perform well enough to feel worthy." If this is your fear, you're constantly waking up in the morning and the scoreboard is negative. No matter what you do, no matter what you achieve or accomplish, you can't move the needle enough to make you wake up the next morning feeling worthy or great about who you are. If you don't feel worthy apart from your performance, you will hide and not attempt your dreams so you can't fail and lose your worth. Or you will constantly try to prove yourself to others. You're going to wear everybody out. You're going to work yourself to death because you have to have more success and greater achievements.

You have shifted directly into second gear. You're defining your life by your mission or by the quality of relationships you have. You need to understand that you can be kind. You can be kind to yourself. You don't have to drive yourself. You're not a taskmaster to yourself. You don't have to earn that worth, because it comes from your identity. You need to downshift into first gear.

Fear Of Being A Bad Person

"I am a bad person." I know it can be hard for you to shift gears and be introspective, but you might be getting these results in your life as a self-fulfilling prophecy. It's self-sabotaging behavior, because when you experience a negative outcome you believe it's what you deserve because you are a bad person.

Why would you believe you're bad? Often, people who have been abused believe this. It's the only way they can reconcile the fact that someone who should have loved and protected them did something awful to them. They believe the lie that it was their fault so the dissonance in their brain could make peace with what happened.

Then you grow up, and this lie shapes the narrative driving you. "I'm a bad person; therefore, bad things are going to happen to me." Or, "I'm going to have to settle for being treated this way. I deserve it." This fear is driving you and you're not able to tap into that internal goodness, the security of your identity. Every time something bad happens to you, you are processing your life through mission and community, and you're forgetting about identity.

Pay attention to how you're processing your life. Reframe. No more proving or hiding.

Fear Of A Bad Outcome

"If I mess up, the worst will happen." If this is your fear, you are afraid that the earth is going to fall out from under you at any moment. There's no secure ground. There's a struggle with anxiety, always waiting for the shoe to drop. Sometimes you will hide behind some sort of religious thinking, or false thinking in your leadership that makes you believe if you do A and B then you will get C. You believe you can master life with a cause-and-effect equation. Whether you become superstitious or rigid, you're looking for certainty that isn't there. You feel like you need a certain outcome to at least feel safe in a dangerous world.

When you process your life along the lines of identity and you understand that you are always internally secure, you do not have to live with the threat that if you mess up the worst will happen. In good times life becomes a playground. You know you will make mistakes. You can embrace the idea of failure. That's the only way you will get to the edge of your abilities and grow. You may have moments when you feel like you fail as a parent or you fail in that initiative at work, but you learn how to put yourself out there and make small bets to get big wins as you grow. In hard times your tenacity or grit is developed. You live resiliently, understanding that external danger becomes an opportunity to develop internal fortitude.

If this fear is dominating you, it shuts your life down. When your life feels shut down you either try to prove it by aggressively micromanaging all the variables, or you crumble under the weight of despair.

Fear Of Vulnerability

"If I'm vulnerable, I'll be hurt." I can sit around a table with a team of executives, male and female, and at some point in their lives each one was hurt by someone powerful. Because of that, they won't be vulnerable. They will either hide and not be who they are or they will prove and be aggressive and push people away. Both tactics block their leadership.

I've seen people ruin both their businesses and the relationships they value, because every time others start to get close to them, they flare up. They pick a fight. Why? Because they will push you away before you have the chance to hurt them. They need an internal awareness of their identity so they can learn gentleness. They need to learn that yes, some people are going to hurt you. You can be wise and intentional about the way you develop relationships and you can develop relationships with people who are going to be safe. Not everyone should be a confidant.

The passive manifestation of this fear is to only reveal the parts of who you are that you think can't get hurt. If you always play devil's advocate or stay silent then you don't have to risk being exposed. Fear will stop driving these responses when you understand that no external pain has to define your identity. Then you can bring full engagement to your mission and your community.

Fear Of Being Replaceable

"I'm nothing special." If we believe we're nothing special, we're constantly on a search to figure out our uniqueness. Fear begins to go deep into our minds. We feel replaceable. We feel like we're just one of seven billion. Maybe we're in a relationship where we're afraid of being replaced. Maybe at work we have even been told directly that we are replaceable.

That pain drives us. We become determined to prove we are special. We double down on our efforts to be the most disciplined and intentional of our peers. We're convinced that enough discipline will mean exceptional results thus securing our place in the world as unique. Sometimes we distract ourselves with regimented discipline afraid to sit with our pain, fears, and desires. We are afraid if we don't rigidly and externally impose discipline then our internal world may confirm that we don't stand out from the pack. Rather than building habits we enjoy we are using the false energy of fear to hype ourselves into regimented change.

Or we learn to comfort the pain of not experiencing our uniqueness through destructive habits. We hide them away and think nobody knows about it. We haven't learned yet how to marshal our energies into making our unique mark. We hide with these habits, or maybe we try to prove that we're not easily replaceable. We may not ever say it out loud, but we operate that way, and we end up pushing people away while proving and hiding. This fear needs the true energy that comes from learning to experience their inner uniqueness.

It's Not About The Paint

Remember, these fears come into our lives through experiences, whether it's a thousand little stings, a few big cuts, or a combination of both. When you get insight on this, you will learn why that movie is your favorite, or why you love those songs. There is a certain kind of narrative you are attracted to. From your preferences to your work to your relationships, everything is a clue. There are people I know who were bullied as kids, so they wanted to be policemen to protect others. That's a good thing. They are trying to give. Others are policemen because they were bullied as kids and they want the power. Fear is driving them.

I want to give you a few exercises to process this information. When my kids were too young to get water for themselves they would ask me for a drink and I would fill up their sippy cups. When they became old enough to fill their own cups we played a game. If they asked me for water, I said, "If you're old enough to get yo water…" in a rhythmic tune. They would respond, "Holla!" I tried to make the experience of getting their own water fun so they would learn to fill their own cups.

Imagine this: One of my daughters, not quite old enough to fill her own cup, asked me for water and I replied, "I can't wait until you're old enough to fill your own sippy cup." What does she hear? "Your needs are a problem." Then when she is 24, being overworked by her boss, she won't feel confident to stand before her boss and explain what she needs because she still believes her needs are a problem.

I use this illustration to demonstrate that there are a thousand little ways—and a few big ones—that this fear narrative is ingrained in you. If you work through the fears, you might feel the weight of all nine. The more time you spend reflecting, you will find a few of them become very clear. Maybe you have already had that experience. Spend time with this. Introspect, wrestle, think. Eventually you will gain deep clarity on what that one fear is for you and you will recognize proving and hiding in the small moments. And if you find yourself dismissing a fear with no plausibility of relating to your story, you might want to take a second look at it. Oftentimes that fear is covered up under your defenses.

In this pursuit of clarity, don't feel pressure to force your way to an answer. Relax with it. It will come when it needs to. Analyze. Sit with it. Don't force it. Stay alert and know that your brain wants to remove dissonance. It wants a story. Your brain will even force a false one to make you feel better. Just to prove the point: Did you know every color of Froot Loops tastes the same? Sorry to ruin your childhood like that. Look it up. It's true. Your brain has been lying to you all these years.

I had a big insight one day. It was during my season of struggle that I referenced in Chapter 1. I came home one day and my wife, who is passionate about decorating our home, said, "Hey, we need to get some paint on this wall." She knew how I was struggling. She wasn't saying it needed to happen right then. She was checking to see if I cared about it too.

It should have been simple for me to affirm her and agree to paint the wall in the future. But this conversation happened when I was in a season of trying to figure out how to buy groceries for the week. So, listening through the filter of my internal insecurity, I heard her say, "You suck as a husband. Can't you get your crap together? Why do I even have to bring this up? I wish I wasn't even married to you." She didn't actually say any of that, but that's what I heard because I was blocked up.

I was hearing her according to the narrative of my fear. For me, the struggle is that if I'm not performing well, then I believe I'm not worthy. I wasn't performing well in my mind, therefore I wasn't worthy; therefore, I was relating out of insecurity and blocking my ability to give her what she needed. Instead, I was trying to get something from her. We almost incited World War III because I was trying to prove that I was doing everything to keep things going, which ignited her fears. Shots were being fired and we weren't even fighting about the wall. It was all about the insecurity of our identities.

Our fear leaves a deep mark on us. You will never be the leader that you can be until you understand your fear.

To begin to understand why the fear is there, we begin by understanding the difference between shame and guilt. Guilt is when you feel bad about what you have done. Shame is when you feel bad about who you are. You are probably familiar with the story of Adam and Eve. In that story, it says that they were naked and felt no shame. The focus is not on physical nudity. It's on being in a space where you never feel bad about who you are, where none of these fears are present. You feel alive and celebrated. You feel congruence. Your mission is the overflow of who you are. Your community is healthy, beautiful, and celebrates you. There's no interaction of fear. Shame communicates a lie to you about who you are. Fear makes you feel the lie of shame. I'm going to lead you to freedom over the course of this book so that you can learn the truth about who you are. So that you can feel, see, and hear that you are loved. So that you can draw from that abundant identity within. Fear and shame are the keys to unlocking this. This story also helps us understand what it's like to go from what is recorded as the height of human existence—a feeling of no shame—to where Adam and Eve actually succumb to this shame. Maybe there's a reason this story has held the attention of many people for thousands of years. Rather than being distracted over arguments of the literal nature of the story we can find ourselves in the metaphor's meaning.

What do Adam and Eve do when they are swallowed up in their shame? They hide. People have followed their lead and fashioned an internal image about who they are through the lens of their own shame. Your internal scorning speech and the visual of what you see towards yourself, whether it's furrowed eyebrows or bad feelings, reveal the shame. If you believe in any kind of sacred power you have done the same with it also. Adam and Eve ran and hid. They made fig leaves to cover up. Why? Because the shame was engulfing them. Then Adam tried to prove it was the woman's fault. The essence of leadership is being aware of your fear. Now that we have a precise awareness of the fears that distract and derail us, we will learn where these fears originate in the next chapter. Zombies aren't real and neither are the fears regarding our identity. But I know it feels that way. We're going to change that.

Exercises To Complete

I want to help you tap into your awareness.

1. Pay attention to what it's like for you to interact with others or for you to interact with your work. Notice at least one moment of proving and hiding and notice one moment of fear. Take a tense, stressful, or frustrating moment and consider what you may have insecurely wanted to prove or hide. The more you can learn to notice this in the smallest of moments the more your brain will attune to deeper awareness. It will create momentum that will cascade into awareness in the big moments. Learn to notice the shame or fear in the fleeting thoughts and small exchanges.

2. For another level of growth, notice your emotional state and record it somewhere. You want to learn to not deny or be dominated by your feelings. You want to learn to use them as energy and clues. Later I will tell you more stories to help with that. For now, notice your emotional state. By noticing, you will learn you can feel opposite emotions at the same time, that negative emotions are momentary and will pass, and you will increase your emotional capacity to feel pain and joy without being driven blindly to act. Start with the simplicity of noticing sad, mad, or glad. From there, explore the nuances and layers of feelings. Stress responses can be buried into our physiology and take 20 years before they manifest themselves. Noticing the proving and hiding now will change your trajectory into the future.

3. For those of you who want to go even deeper with it, walk back through each of the nine fears. Read those sections again and take some notes. I'm not saying the aliens that started the human race wrote these on a cave wall for us to find, but there is some ancient wisdom in those fears.* The more you contemplate this, the more you will recognize when you're proving and hiding. These fears work like an onion. You

may feel parts of many of them but you want to peel back to the core.

4. Evaluate behavioral changes you have made in your life. Any behavioral change attempted through shame deforms your identity and will not last. If you look over these fears and start shaming yourself, please know you can't shame yourself into change. There's a difference between sitting with the pain and punishing yourself.

CHAPTER THREE LEARN YOUR STORY

It takes more courage to examine the dark corners of your own soul than it does for a soldier to fight on a battlefield.

W.B. YEATS

We shrink back to hide or power up to prove because we are insecure.

Hiding and proving will not fix the problems you are facing right now. Hiding or proving simply masks the deeper problem and makes them worse for you and those around you. As I looked at my own journey and contemplated this, I realized I had been ignoring the stuff that needed my attention.

Several years ago, I went canoeing with a friend down a river known for its whitewater rapids. It was like being in a giant pinball machine. I think we flipped our canoe every single time we hit a rapid. After the first day, the outfitter was pretty upset about the condition of his boat. For the protection of his equipment, he decided to give us some instruction on how to get through the rapids. He climbed into the boat and positioned his center of gravity really low. He said, "Every time you come to the rocks, you're instinct is going to be to lean away from them. When you lean away from the rocks the water shoots into your boat and causes it to flip. Tomorrow, every time you come to a rock, lean towards it."

The next day on the river, my friend and I heeded that advice. Resisting our instincts to lean away from the dreaded rocks, we yelled at each other to help us fight our gut reaction to pull away. I wish you could have heard us yelling. "Lean in! Lean in! Lean in!" Each time we approached a rock, we leaned into it, shooting through the rapids with precision. By following the flow of the water and leaning into the rocky places, we were able to return the canoe to the outfitter without any damage.

What you're not paying attention to or leaning into is getting in your way. It's why you commit self-sabotaging behavior and why you can't form deep connections with people. This is also the reason why you can't lead the team to either embrace a new initiative or openly process why they don't agree with it. We need to learn how to lean in. This will allow us to learn our story.

Imagine if you were to stand in front of your team meeting today and announce to everyone, "I want you to know when we start talking about certain initiatives, I tend to power up and try to control the conversation," or, "When we face tough decisions I usually start to fidget and hide because I don't want to go deep into that topic." No one on your team would be surprised. If I were to ask my wife, "Did you know when I'm overcommitted, I start to get uptight and frustrated at little things?" She's not going to say, "I don't know what you mean." These people are already seeing your behavior. It's time for you to see it.

The places you prove and hide are already obvious to others. Don't miss what's obvious to everyone else. If a skilled biographer were to help you analyze the timeline of your life, they could help you gain an awareness of cause-and-effect trigger points you have never noticed before. This is what I want to help you learn to do. This is what I mean by "learn your story."

A War Of Voices

As you learn your story and pay attention to what's happening, you're going to notice a war of voices within yourself. I want you to pay attention to that. I know it sounds weird, but stay with me. You can break it down if you think about it as three competing voices: the voice that pressures you to project, the voice of shame, and the voice of who you are. I am not saying these are audible voices, but pressures at an intuitive level. Let me be your trail guide on this and see if it matches your experience.

The first voice is the part of ourselves that we want to project to others. We want to make people think something about us. This is the proving or hiding. We're trying to control their perception of us. Our internal chatter in this voice is constantly consumed with what others think.

The second voice is a shaming narrator. We end up being driven by a false story that we feel we have to live up to. Whether or not we are aware of it, the narrator is harnessing voices from our past that spoke in a voice of shame. We talked about shame in the previous chapter. Shame is when you feel like you will never have a place where you are accepted and can feel at home. We have an image we want to project (the first voice) because this internal narrative of shame (the second voice) is driving us. The image we want to project by proving or hiding isn't who we really are. The driving narration of shame isn't who we are. Both of these voices are clues and signals to who we are. We need to learn why the shame is there and where it came from so it will stop blocking the truest expression of who we are and thus the uniqueness of our leadership.

We want to find our third voice: who we are. Who we are at our core is free of the pressure and the shame.

How are you going to do that? How are you going to separate the image shame drives you to project from who you actually are? The answer is simple but difficult to practice for especially high performers: Pay attention to your emotional state.

Emotions Are Messages And Clues

Most people dismiss this quickly. We have been taught that feelings are terrible liars, that they will put a lid on your leadership, that you have to lead and tell your feelings where to follow. Frankly, shutting down your feelings can help you rack up achievements. But when you do that to yourself, you condition yourself into a numbed-out state. You bury stress responses. You miss your brilliance. Your subconscious mind is ready to aid and assist you with creativity and energy. It is far more brilliant and has more information than your conscious mind. "Feelings" are the communication language of the subconscious to the conscious.

Additionally, when you fail to lead from the humanity of your experience, other people will not whole-heartedly follow your leadership because they are human and they have feelings. You won't create momentum or energy. Vulnerability gives energy; pretending drains it.

This isn't about over sharing or pushing people away by being draining. It's about knowing your emotional state and how to pay attention to it. The more you know and pay attention to your emotional state, the more your work and leadership will flow from an authentic place, and the more you will be able to pay attention to others and lead in a healthy and empowered way. You have to tell yourself, "I'm not going to be dominated by my emotions, nor am I going to deny them. I'm going to be aware and learn, because my emotions are critical clues for me." I have learned to pay attention and lean in. I have learned to look people in the eyes and see them for who they are and where they are. The more I do that with myself and the more I do that with others, the more I'm able to be emotionally intelligent for them and for myself.

All leadership is a journey. You're on a journey. I'm on a journey. You're taking your organization on a journey. How do you know how to get to your destination if you don't know where you are right now? Part of knowing where you are is an emotional assessment of things. You can force the new initiative down everyone's throats, but you won't get a healthy culture, whole-hearted effort, or accountability to achieve results. Instead, you will get passive support.

At one point in my career I had taken over a team that was used to a highly dysfunctional leader. The team had grown so fear-driven that nobody felt safe to disagree with the team leader for fear of recompense. But we all know what happens in cultures like that. If the displeasure is not voiced in the meeting, it's being voiced somewhere else. I had been pleading with the team to be honest. The previous leader led by fear. I was trying to lead differently.

It didn't happen in the first meeting, but eventually someone actually called one of the new ideas stupid. I started clapping. He was honest and I wanted our team to know we celebrate honesty. He was honest by saying "stupid." Maybe we could make a change, or maybe we would still have to go with the initiative as it was. I wanted to create an environment in our meetings where we could be completely honest about what we felt. We could leave the room and support the initiative even if we couldn't change the direction from the top. But the support would be more authentic now that the protest had been voiced. Buried protests lead to coups.

An insecure leader whose idea is called "stupid" will either try to shut down the criticism or run from it; proving or hiding. Instead, I paid attention to what was happening inside of me and what was happening in the room. I was aware and learning.

Don't only think about your leadership at work. It's your leadership in all of your life.

This is an embarrassing story to tell, but it's real life. I punched a door in front of my kids. It wasn't because there was something between my kids and me. It was a weak, insecure moment during an argument with my wife. I acted out to try to prove something about myself and handled it in an immature way. Overwhelmed with shame as a dad and as a husband, I went outside and cried. I felt completely defeated.

I talked to my kids about it hours later, processing it with them. I said, "It's not bad to feel strong emotion, but it's unwise to always act on it. Sometimes you feel a strong emotion and you need to act on it, and sometimes you don't need to act on it. Dad acted on this emotion in an immature way. It was okay for me to feel what I was feeling, but I should not have acted out the way I did."

I want you to start thinking about where you're at. Think of it like taking your "emotional temperature" at different points throughout the day.

When I work with clients one-on-one, I have them capture some moments where they feel threatened or afraid and start deconstructing those. One of the things you can use to start making sense of your reactions is what we talked about before. All the times we feel falsely threatened in our identity are because of some part of our story that's unfolding, some narrative of fear we have learned in the past. After we start paying attention to our emotional state we start to clearly see where our false narratives originated. When you look back over the trajectory of your life, what are your top five hurts? What are moments where your life shifted or experiences that shaped you? Often, it's these big moments that reinforce lots of small interactions. They are often caused because children are great recorders but terrible interpreters. These incorrect interpretations often reinforce the lies we began to believe about who we are. Our lives are shaped by experiences, but for most of us, we have never paid attention to them. We never learned our story.

You can't figure out who you are until you have assessed what you have been through. This isn't about paying attention to your past by obsessing over it or feeling defined by it. Your history is not your identity. Your identity is more true and more real than even the thoughts you have about yourself right now or the emotions you feel. Who you are is solid and secure. But to get to that, you have to look at the experiences that have shaped you. As you start to look at these themes, you will be able to connect them back to the fears we talked about in Chapter 2. You're looking for places where the needs of your identity may have been actively violated or passively neglected.

When we start to process this, the light bulbs click on. It may take some time, but the more we lean into our emotions, connect them to the past and asses what we have been through, the more present and aware we become. This is the process of learning our own story.

Perhaps you have trouble getting to a place where you feel. For a lot of us, we feel numb. We have conditioned ourselves through some sort of habit or practice—you could call it an addiction or compulsion—and we have developed patterns of shutting down what we feel. Typically, an addiction is behavior that spirals out of control because an ever-bigger "hit" is required. A compulsion is a behavior we turn to that we wish we could stop. Both are done to suppress pain and avoid leaning in. If you feel numb, you need to identify and stop giving in to the compulsion or addiction. It could be obsession over work. It could be something that our culture would celebrate like a committed relationship that veils codependency. It could be a thousand different things, but whatever it is we need to identify what we run to for comfort when we feel afraid. Most people aren't even aware that they're running to it. As we become aware and stop running to it, the pain comes to the surface and we can process it.

Emotional intelligence is a phrase that's tossed around a lot. Another way I like to say it is "aware and learning." This isn't optional. If you aren't aware and learning emotionally, your relationships will be blocked up, your sense of focus and clarity in mission will be off-kilter, and your ability to connect with and engage the team will be absent. Stop whatever you're running to, let the pain come to the surface, and start paying attention to it and processing it.

Find someone you can talk to about what's happening, someone who you don't have to posture and pretend with. Don't talk about it factually or in a way to influence their thinking about the events. Instead, get to that colorful level of language where it's visceral and you feel it. Maybe you have to write it out. Take one of those hurts and write a letter to someone about it without sending it. Feel it. Up to this point the pain, the hurts, and the lies have all shaped your response in your leadership. You need to learn your story, even the painful parts.

But Your Brain Can Trick You

I could not imagine a more embarrassing first time out with my future in-laws. A chunk of food got caught in my throat. My girlfriend's dad sprang into action and did the Heimlich. It didn't work. I gagged myself in the middle of the restaurant and dislodged the food. Gross humiliation. A little backstory: In sixth grade, I choked on a piece of KFC chicken. My dad had to do the Heimlich on me. I remember very vividly the way the chicken shot out of my mouth and across Colonel Sanders' dining area. I still remember my sixth grade self being completely mortified. Of course, it doesn't take much to embarrass a sixth grader who desperately wants to be cool.

From that moment on, me and food had an uneasy relationship. About once a year food gets stuck in my throat and I have to work to dislodge it. I have learned to leave the table, run to the bathroom and deal with it. That strategy worked for me until one night when I fixed a steak to celebrate finishing a massive project. A piece of steak lodged itself in my throat. It wouldn't budge. I was completely panicked. In the past I would simply jump up from the table and take care of it while my wife and kids had been conditioned to remain calm and wait for me to come out of the bathroom.

Not this time. I locked eyes with my wife and she could tell that this was different. It was an emergency. She ran out the back door to find our neighbor, a retired EMT. I ran to the bathroom and desperately tried to dislodge the meat from my throat so I could breathe again.

I finally managed to dislodge the piece of meat and reassured my wife that everything was okay. With crying children in the background, she gave me a look. With one look she told me she and the kids had put up with this trauma long enough so I visited a doctor. During the case history review with the ENT doctor, he told me if food was actually getting stuck in my airway I wouldn't be able to dislodge it because it would go into my lung. Since the sixth grade, whenever I felt like something was stuck, it would trigger me to relive the traumatic incident.

The doctor said your brain can actually trick you into thinking you can't breathe. You would pass out, but you would simply wake back up because you would start breathing again. My mind was blown. Every time I thought I was choking, I wasn't. Since I learned that, every time food has gotten stuck, I have repeated to myself, "You're still breathing, it's going to be okay." Because I stay relaxed, it goes down.

My brain was reacting based on a completely false understanding because of trauma. There are reactions that you're having that are based on completely false understandings of who you are. In small and big ways you have been actively hurt and passively neglected. Those small and big events have conditioned you. Your brain is tricking you. I'll teach you how to train your brain in Chapter 7. For now I want to make sure you understand that past pain in your life is causing your brain to force a false narrative regarding your identity. The reason you believe a lie about who you are is because the pain you have experienced traumatized you to suffocate under the voice of shame. Shame blocks the voice of who you are.

A Note About Blaming Yourself And Blaming Others

This isn't about putting anyone on trial, including yourself. Where there's blame there's shame. I've seen it many times. An older parent starts to shed tears. Shame sets in. They are condemning themselves for skipping over identity in parenting or marriage or a relationship they valued. Suddenly the out-of-nowhere rebellious behavior makes sense. Suddenly the marriage that never seemed to work is now seen as two insecure people fighting to meet the needs of their identity. You can repair the tear. It doesn't mean the relationship can be saved. You both may have moved on, but you can grieve and let go of the false defensiveness. You can reach out to your lost children. You can start validating their heart rather than stressing over their performance. It will take a long time to rebuild trust but it can be done.

This is also not about blaming others. They could only give what they had. They couldn't give security because they were insecure in their identity. But you now have permission to feel, see, and hear the active and passive wounds. While we want perfect caretaking, none of us gets that. Now you can explain the poor caretaking you received without excusing it.

You may need to confront someone, but before you do, grieve it out. How much or how often do you need to grieve it? You don't have to constantly look backward. Look forward through the windshield. If the pain is obstructing a clear view then grieve it out. Express your sadness. Express your sadness as often as it pops up on your windshield. Learn to be a safe place for yourself. The more you can give yourself permission to fall apart and put yourself back together the more you will be a safe, sane, and stable place for others. In the coming chapters I'll teach you how.

Do you want to learn who you are? Learn your story. Do you want to learn your story? Start looking at what's happening in you emotionally. A good place to begin connecting the dots is your past. As you uncover more and more of the truth of who you are, it will unleash desires within you so that you can figure out what you want to do in the world and who you want to be as a person. Those are rapids you don't have to be afraid of. Lean in. In some way, lean in and pay attention to what's happening.

Exercises To Complete

If you stay engaged in these exercises you will learn:

- How to build a narrative of your life. Find the plot twists and defining moments.
- That all behavior has meaning. What actions have come out of the pain?
- To process honestly what happened.

1. List the top five hurts you have experienced. What theme or themes are present? (What are your favorite movies, books, or songs? Often there is a connection to this theme. Art surfaces the depths of who we are. The song can be an expression of grief that we identify with or an expression of hope for what we want.) Often things occur in childhood that shape our responses for years to come. Those responses helped us survive in the past but will cause us harm in the future.

2. 2. Take one of the five moments and if it involves only you then write

a letter to yourself about it. If it involves someone else, write a letter to them. Filter nothing. Emotionalize. The act of writing with pen on paper is visceral and will help unblock what is stuck. By the way, don't send it.

3. The recovery movement uses the saying, "H.A.L.T. before you mess up." When you're H.ungry, A.ngry, L.onely, or T.ired you are more likely to make poor decisions. We all have compulsions or addictions. We use them to quiet the pain. Stop the compulsion or addiction and allow the pain to come to the surface. Look for the moments you feel afraid, lonely, angry, or worn down and watch to see what action you turn to for comfort.

Additional questions to stir up what might be buried:
What have you done in your life to be near or feel near to your father or mother?

What do you do now or avoid doing to be away from him or her (even if it's a memory of them)?

Can you listen for the ways you might misunderstand or judge the 18-year-old version of yourself who was holding it together (or whatever age you struggled liking yourself)?

CHAPTER FOUR

FLIP THE LIE

The dark does not destroy the light;
it defines it. It's our fear of the dark
that casts our joy into the shadows.

BRENE BROWN

When walking through fear, shame and pain, it's normal to feel like you're drowning. Identifying problems isn't very fun when they're your own problems. But until you know how to recognize your insecurity in the smallest moments, you'll never see the changes you want to see in the big moments. At this point it might feel like I have turned up the volume of your shame. Let me assure you that the shame is not screaming louder; you're learning to hear. That's exactly where you want to be.

Why is it important to learn to hear the voice of shame? Because shame has a terrible poker face. It will tell you precisely the lie you believe. Once you learn to identify shame's lie, you can flip that lie. Flipping anything – tables, chairs, coins – sounds fun, so let's hone in on your lie.

Like a detached observer we'll learn to notice the lie we falsely believe about our identity and flip it to its opposite conclusion. When you become aware of any of the identity fears, you can flip the lie because you are not defined by mission or community. The darkness of your identity fear defines the light of who you really are.

Disordered And Defeated

If we don't learn to flip our lies, we're going to make terrible choices out of insecurity. We will not be able to overflow our best leadership. We will not be able to pay attention to emotional cues. We will not be able to lean into moments where we could turn bad into good. We will be numb, we will self-sabotage, and we will be our own worst enemy. Our internal world will be disordered and we will feel defeated.

Flipping the lie requires more introspection on your part. I'm going to teach you a progression of how to recognize instances when you believe a lie in the smallest moments. To do so, we need to return to the big idea from

Chapter 1. We talked about identity, mission, and community. Think of it as a progression visualized here:

Identity > Mission > Community

When you're secure in who you are, you will overflow a clear mission and build healthy community. Who you are shapes what you do and the relationships you build.

Disorder occurs when you're living with a false identity, you're living with a false mission, so you pretend in your community. This progression will give you insight into the small moments when you're insecure:

False self > False Mission > False Community
Hurts > Inadequacies > Pretenses
Prove/Hide > Frustration > Judgments

When you're hurt in who you are, you will feel inadequate in what you do. Whenever you feel inadequate in who you are, you will pretend in your community. When you prove or hide within yourself, then you will be frustrated in your mission and be judgmental towards your community. If someone is afraid, they will either passively resign or aggressively power up. If someone is frustrated in figuring out the focus of their mission, there is insecurity in their identity that blocks up living from their true desires. If you meet someone who's judgmental, you know you're interacting with someone who's very insecure.

Hurts in our identity will result in being frustrated in our mission. This isn't about frustration at obstacles but the restlessness within when our doing isn't aligned with our being. When we live out of a secure identity, our mission may change. We may realize our current commitments were birthed out of a false motivation and a different passion may rise to the surface. For others, the mission may not change. Instead, we may experience newfound motivation within the same work. Consider the fireman who rescues people to feel worthy and then learns he is already worthy. Now he can rescue simply to help people. The motive changes. He works to give something to others, not to get something from it.

Don't get me wrong. It's fine for him to feel good about his good deeds, but if getting the good feeling drives him, he is only rescuing to get. That feeling of needing to get something from what you do signifies a false mission. At some point, his identity will collapse under the weight of needing to rescue people to feel whole. True mission, or mission that is overflow from a secure being, is striving to give something because you already have abundant security within.

You can do the same thing with your community. We all know people who are only in relationships to get something. We feel drained every time we are around them. The hard part is noticing when we are doing the exact same thing. In my closest relationships with my wife, my daughters, and my friends I definitely get things: support, love, companionship, and encouragement. Those are all good things. But I become a draining person when my default mindset is to get something from them. I'm human, so of course there are moments when I slip into that mode, but relationships hit the next level when we learn to engage out of overflow, rather than need. Comedian George Carlin had a comically true bit about how anyone who drives faster than you is a maniac and anyone who drives slower is an idiot. You have the perception that you know the perfect speed to drive. People compare in every category of life. "Have you seen the size of their house? Do they need that much space?" or "They should take better care of their house. Don't they want to care for their investment?" From parenting to health and lifestyle choices we have mastered the "perfect standard" of how things should be done. The rest of the human race would be so lucky to be more like us.

In our family's growth, there came a point where I realized my family needed more of my help around the house. I started taking more initiative on helping with household chores like laundry, vacuuming and dishes. One night I was loading the dishwasher, and my wife was in the next room unable to clearly see how great of a husband I was being. Being pretty savvy, I got her attention by clinking the dishes together until she thanked me. I wasn't washing dishes to help out or give something to her, I was doing it to get worth and affirmation from her. The nuance is subtle, but powerful. We talked about fears in Chapter 2. My fear is that I'm not worthy unless I perform well. I did the dishes so I could get a celebration of performance. I was trying to live out of third gear—community. I was trying to get something from my relationships. I want to live out of first gear—identity—where I don't need anything from my community to feel whole. So even if I'm not noticed, I will still do the dishes. And if it is noticed, that's a bonus. I get to enjoy that celebration, but my worth isn't defined by it.

Most people never notice these subtleties within because they aren't aware of where they feel insecure in their identity. We believe a lie of shame about who we are based on the hurts of life, which leads to inadequacies in our mission and pretenses in our community. We start comparing ourselves to others, so we are energized to respond out of an insecure identity. Learning to recognize the false self in the small moments will help you learn to flip the lie. A few years ago we bought bicycles for our daughters for Christmas. Like a smart Santa, I hid them in my neighbor's garage. On Christmas Eve we loaded the bikes into my van. Let me tell you, it would have been easier to use a big red bag and a sleigh. Our van had a broken hinge on the trunk, so I had to lean the door on my back as we loaded the bikes. Watching me struggle to make this work, my neighbor said, "That's dangerous. Your family could get hurt." Feeling the stinging accusation of his words, I told him I had an appointment the following week to fix the hinge.

I didn't have an appointment the next week. I didn't have an appointment the next month. I didn't have an appointment at all! It was a stupid little lie, but it was a big red flag about my condition. I was pretending in my community because I felt insecure. I wanted to prove that I had it all together. I wanted to hide the truth. An inconsequential white lie served as a strong clue about my insecurity.

We live lies more than we tell them.

Ordered And Resilient

What do our lives look like when we flip the lie? I want you to remember the paradigm of identity, mission, and community.

Secure identity > True Mission > Healthy Community
Aware > Flip > Give
Peace > Passion > Understanding

The first step to living from a secure identity - to be able to flow brilliantly in a moment - is being aware. This awareness is discovering the fear, shame, and pain. The more attuned you are to the pain, the more you learn when you're numbing out. The more you resist numbing out, the more beautiful and brilliant all of your life will become.

One evening - after a long day working - my daughter came downstairs and slid me a note. I was learning to resist my own numbing. I was stunned as I read the note: "Will you dance with me?" I experienced a wave of gratitude, joy, and beauty that I can only describe as "full presence". As I danced with her, it was one of the first deeply present moments I had ever felt as a father. I felt peace in who I was. I felt passion in my role. I felt understanding towards here in way that is difficult to put into words. As I was learning to pay attention to fear, shame, and pain, I was able to feel peace in a deeper way. The more you notice the pain the more you can notice the joy.

After you're aware you flip the lie. Is it really true that we never have a place to belong? Is it really true that we'll never have a place where we're safe? In our identity, no outside force can define or take away from who we are. Take your fear and flip it.

The more aware you are of your fear, shame, pain, and lies, the more you will be aware of what's happening in others' lives. You flip the lie and then you give to your community.

When you follow this progression of aware-flip-give, you'll feel peace in who you are. There will be resilient passion in your mission. Resiliency comes when you separate who you are from what you do. You can keep going regardless of the results or stop doing things that don't need repeated because you're not attached to your doing. You know who you are separate from your doing and have peace in that. You have passion in your mission and understanding in your community. You're able to look around and understand why people do what they do.

It takes your leadership to a sophisticated place because you're able to give empathy and still be strategic where you need to be. You can give understanding and lead them well. This isn't about cognitive willpower and forcing your way through the problem, it's about learning a different way of thinking.

It was a few weeks before Christmas, and I came home to find our kitchen sink leaking. I didn't want to deal with it because I had a lot going on with work. Plus, it was right before Christmas and I didn't want to spend money on it. But the leak was getting worse. I went to the hardware store and had an idea. I would apply silicone spray to momentarily stop the leak.

If you know anything about plumbing, you're probably thinking I'm an idiot. And you would be right. I'm terrible at fixing things. But I was at the hardware store explaining what I wanted to do, and the guy said, "That sounds like it will work." So I got the silicone spray and sprayed it inside where the leak was occurring, and the leak mostly stopped. I thought I fixed the problem.

I came home a few days before Christmas and there was a puddle of water in the basement, right under the sink. My attempt to fix the problem with intensity made it worse because I didn't fix it with clarity.

Most of us start to figure some things out about our leadership and maybe how we're not getting the results we want, and we apply some intensity—

maybe to the people around us, maybe to ourselves, telling them we should try harder and do better. Unfortunately, it's like being in a boat on autopilot headed south and wanting to go north. So you turn north. But you can only hold the direction for so long. The autopilot will outlast all your efforts. You can apply all the intensity you want, but eventually you will get tired and let go, and the boat will turn back south. Moving forward we you will learn how to program a new autopilot. You will learn how to live from a new baseline. But you need clarity in the small moments when you are living insecure. It starts with understanding in the smallest moments when you're living a lie. Where are you proving, hiding, frustrated, or judging? Notice it. Be aware. Flip the lie. Give.

Shame's poker face is now your advantage.

Exercise To Complete:

1. Go on a walk. You'll need to have a pen with you. As you're moving, ask yourself, "Is there a lie that I believe about who I am?" That's going to be the hurt. That's going to be the part where you want to prove or hide, because this is what you need clarity on. Look around for any symbol that brings meaning, hope, clarity, anger, or peace regarding the lie. It can symbolize the lie or hope that the lie doesn't define you. If it is something you can carry take the symbol with you.

2. Then I want you to find a stick. Write that lie on your stick, and then break the stick. Or burn the stick. Or maybe you want to write it out as a letter and burn the letter. Build a ritual that is meaningful to you. You can be a cynic and hide from the vulnerability of this moment. Or let it impact you and your neural networks by emotionalizing it. Feel it. Break it. Scream if you need to. Run. Breath. Feel. Do something that in a visceral way helps you ceremonially welcome yourself to a new epoch or era of being you.

   Societies and religions relish rituals because we need these moments of passage. We need moments that help us close off one era and start a new one. Society used to have rituals built in for the different stages of identity development. You would leave the village a boy. Sleep in the dark cave. Come back a man. You can build your own rituals. So break that stick, burn that letter, and close off that era of living suffocated under the lie.

CHAPTER FIVE WRITE A NEW ENDING

The unhappy person is one who has his ideal,
the content of his life, the fullness of his consciousness,
the essence of his being, in some manner outside of himself.
The unhappy man is always absent from himself,
never present to himself.

SOREN KIERKEGAARD

I have a confession: I have always hated things described as "self-help." To me, most motivational stuff feels like hype and BS. I can't count the number of times I've taken meticulous notes at an event only to file those notes away to collect dust and never to be referenced again. Despite those disappointments, I know this: motivation can be centering and lasting. It doesn't have to be temporary hype. We don't need motivation that's so fleeting we forget it by the time we answer the next email. We want a new baseline, a new wiring, so we can learn to lead from an abundant mindset. The only way you can really get lasting motivation is by intentionally unlocking desire. Desire flows from a deeper, more sustainable source than external motivation.

There's a difference between managing employees and successfully leading employees. I can spend all day managing employee agreements related to what their responsibilities are, but I don't want to manage people. I want to lead them. How do I do that? How do you do that? By tapping into your employee's desire.

I want my team to be honest about their desire so we can focus toward where their desires will lead them anyway. I'm sure you have had employees that keep running in the direction they want to, not where you need them to go. They are probably in the wrong role. You have to align them with their internal desire. If you want to help others, you need to unblock your desires at the deepest levels and stop judging yourself.

To quickly gain clarity on your desires, you need to write a new ending. I want you to write a new ending on your work, life, and relationships. As children, we are always asked what we want to do when we grow up. No one ever asks who we want to become. No one ever asks that question from a character standpoint. Imagine if someone had asked you as a child what you want to do when you grow up and you responded, "Well, I don't know exactly what I want to do and I'll probably try lots of things, but I want to be adventurous, generous, and fully present for all of life's experiences." They would have been stunned and speechless. We search for certainty in our mission or community but we can only have certainty in choosing who we become.

Up to this point, I have given you a way of understanding your identity based on three competing pressures: who you really are, the image you want to project to others, and the lies you believe about who you are because of fear and shame. These pressures make up the cloudy and diluted concoction of who you are. If you can think about these three pressures as opposing voices it will help you learn to hear your voice the loudest.
To help you understand desire, think about your identity in the context of these three competing voices: the voice of tradition, the voice of others, and the internal voice of your desires.*

Most people have a keen sense of what they "should" do. There are traditions in our lives that drive our choices and shape what we believe about the world or ourselves. Occasionally, there is a relationship with someone who exerts a lot of influence—another leader or a parent—who becomes the strong voice of another. This influential person may hold a position of authority in our lives or may exude a manipulative interpersonal presence. Tradition and the strong presence of another can hold so much power over our lives that the pressure of "should" blocks us from knowing who we are and what we really want.

Let The Desires Rage

You cannot lead from a solid and secure core until you understand your desires. We have to be honest about what we like and what we don't like. For a lot of us, we don't actually know what are our true desires are because the strong voice of tradition and the strong voice of another overwhelm our ability to know what we really want.

When my kids played softball, all the parents had to serve a rotation working the snack shack at the games. I hated it. The snack shack was positioned where the volunteers couldn't see much of the game from behind the counter. I didn't want to spend my Saturday morning serving watered down beverages and lukewarm hot dogs. I wanted to watch my daughter play softball. As I passed food over the counter and collected money, I would crane my neck around the corner to see if my daughter was up to bat. I didn't do a good job in the snack shack because it's not where my heart was. My desire was to watch my daughter, not serve snacks. I believe everyone, even if they had the wealth to never work again, needs a sense of purpose and mission in their work. But the work has to be built on a secure identity. We will never have a true mission until we're secure in who we are. When we get our desire for identity met then we can be honest about our desires for mission. We have to figure out who we are and what we want so we're not 40 years old and still stuck in the snack shack while our heart is on the softball field.

During a recent ride to the airport, I struck up a conversation with the Uber driver. He had just graduated from college and was embarking on his next degree to become a dentist. Through the discussion about our career paths, he revealed that he really wanted to be a carpenter. He was only taking the route to dentistry for the potential income. It seems absurd, doesn't it? Investing all that time and money into a degree that doesn't take him any closer to what he truly wants to do. I told him if he really wanted to be a carpenter he should start now. He should email all his friends and offer to complete three small projects if they pay for the wood. Take on as many projects as your time and energy allow. Commit to doing exceptional work and word of mouth will spread and grow the business over time. His response: "But I'm just so afraid."

It's fear that holds us back. We spent so much time in the previous chapters becoming aware of fear and shame because that is foundational. If you know your deepest desires true to who you are you can stay in growth mode. You are guided in present choices. Should you make a change or persevere? Do you want to stay in that relationship or have the courage to walk away? Have you always wanted your life to look like it does right now or were there subtle pressures that drove you?

I remember when my wife and I moved into what I thought was our dream home. High windows in our great room with remote control blinds, tile turned at an angle, five zones for the stereo system, and a deck wrapped around a big tree in the backyard were going to give me a great feeling of accomplishment. I pushed hard to get there. I remember sitting on the deck and thinking, "This is it? This is what I worked so hard for?" My wife and I could have the same argument whether the countertops were granite or not. I thought my desire was for a new home with all the features. But I really wanted to feel good about myself through accomplishments. Yet, the accomplishment of the home couldn't meet the desire of my identity. My deepest desire was to have my identity fear comforted.

What are your desires? Let's explore that question. Take a pen and paper and write down what you want. Hold nothing back. Write it all out.

Just like we talked about emotions—we don't deny them, but we're not dominated by them—do the same with your desires. What do you want in your relationships? You might want something that's destructive and unhealthy. Write that down. You are of no help to yourself if you ignore that desire. What do you want in your leadership? Maybe you want to lead a company with a certain market cap and a certain number of employees and you want to be worshiped as the top dog. Don't judge yourself. It's normal at this point to have some dark desires surface. While it may be wrong to act on some of them, we need to surface them so we can get underneath what's happening. Pay attention to when you want to run away and make bad choices.

Get Underneath The Desires

Recently, I had a fleeting thought where I wanted to run away from stress and responsibilities. By getting underneath that desire, I was able to acknowledge that I needed to make some changes and rest. Another time I had a quick fantasy thought about a person I didn't know admiring me for all that I could teach them. Underneath that desire I realized I wanted to be celebrated for performing so I could have more worth. Rather than being insecure and needing to teach, I decided to look for places I could learn. In both of those instances, I could only start the process of change by accepting where I was. If you can learn to go inward when you want to go outward, then fleeting thoughts become energizing and directing thoughts. If you could run away right now and be free of responsibility, you would be surprised to find your problems follow. You don't have to attach yourself to your fleeting thoughts. You are more than your thoughts. Change your relationship to your thoughts by learning to study them and your self-talk like a detached researcher. Some thoughts you let pass. Some you study. The guide to know which action to take is by noticing your desires.

This is a state of being most people never reach. They don't introspect because it's painful. They numb out to survive instead. Even if they could be honest about their desires, many would scornfully judge themselves back into proving and hiding. The problem is that they never learn to tap into who they really are. The foundation of a secure identity is radical acceptance of who you are no matter the desires. Even the dark parts of our desires are in some way connected to the desire for love, belonging, acceptance, and safety. Shame is never helpful.

You need to be aware of your desires. Don't deny, don't filter, don't suppress. Keep digging and expose the desires that are inside of you. Put the book down for a moment and write down everything you desire.
Look at those desires you just wrote down. Ask yourself, "Why do I want

these?" How are those desires connected to your story? Maybe some of them reflect a compulsion to be near your father or mother by following in their footsteps and doing something that they did. Those desires reflect the strong voice of tradition and the influential voice of others. Maybe your desires are based on your need to reject the voice of tradition and influential voices of others that are pressuring you to conform. If so, there is an energy in you that says, "None of that will ever be true about me." This brings us to motive. You're not just aware of the desire, you're aware of why you desire it. Motives reveal the real you. Knowing our motives allows us to move past the pretending we all do with ourselves.

Next, I'll show you how to meet the main desire in your identity. Then the mission and community desires can rage. You can pursue the greatness of craftsmanship without pretending or shrinking back. When your identity is free of the oppression of perfectionism, you can unleash a healthy ambition. No more snack shack for you.

Exercise To Complete:

1. Make sure you wrote out your desires.

2. This may seem a little weird to think about, but I want you to consider how people will describe you at your funeral. Remember, this is about identity. It's not what people say you did, it's who people say you are. I want you to tell yourself three stories, or preferably write them out.

   People at your funeral are looking at the pictures on the memory board. A coworker sees a picture of the two of you, a family member sees a picture of the two of you and a friend sees a picture of the two of you. All three of them are reminiscing about who you are. What do they say? Write out three stories.

   I have the three stories in my head around these three groups of people and what characteristics stand out to them when they see these pictures. My family would say that I was present. Those that experience our business would say we are generous. Our team would say that I was adventurous. Those are my three things. This allows me to make decisions at a high level, quickly. I organize my life around these values. You have time to pick yours. You get to choose who you become.

   For these exercises, recall the fear narrative we discussed in Chapter 2. Allow it to shape your stories. These scenarios aren't about recalling facts or influencing anyone. They are about understanding who you are. This is how you write a new ending.

The more you learn your desires, the more you will be able to help those you lead on their journey of desire, whether it is an employee, friend, or family member. Do this not only for yourself and for your leadership, but also do it for others. You are going to add an incredible amount of meaning to the lives of people around you.

CHAPTER SIX TRAIN THE BRAIN

One can think of ordinary, real time as a horizontal line. On the left, one has the past, and on the right, the future. But there's another kind of time in the vertical direction. This is called imaginary time, because it is not the kind of time we normally experience. But in a sense, it is just as real, as what we call real time.

STEPHEN HAWKING

Bad reactions are built on false threats. What would your life look and feel like if you no longer believed your identity could be threatened? Fear and shame would lose its grip on you, no longer driving you to prove and hide. If you don't reframe your state of mind, fear and insecurity will continue to taint your work and your relationships. These fears and insecurities have transformed you into a worse version of yourself.

So far I have tried to help you become aware of fear and pain, to pay attention to the patterns of hurt in your life. This is the first step because of how the human brain works. Your brain has taken note of your past experiences to shape your present response.

Now we need to talk about the brain and understand how it can work either for us or against us. We will learn that our experiences continually shape our brain, thus they continually shape us. We want to learn how we engage those experiences.

In Chapter 1 we addressed the idea of processing everything through identity first. That's why when you engage in conflict, you feel as though you're being attacked for who you are. It's this false threat to your identity that causes you to become insecure in the components that make up who you are. We want to pay attention to the framework we use to engage and understand it better, which will allow us to position ourselves in such a way that our experiences can shape our identity in a healthy way.

Imagine you go into a board meeting this week and everyone has water balloons ready to fire at you. As soon as you walk through the door, you are pelted. This isn't a friendly interaction full of laughter. There is a sentiment of angst. What's going to happen next time you go to the board meeting? You'll poke your head timidly around the corner before entering. You'll be afraid. You'll be skittish. Why? A neural construct formed in reaction to your first experience of entering the meeting. Your brain wants to protect you from future pain, constantly reformulating itself based on experiences that are happening to you and around you. Your brain will tell you that entering the boardroom might end badly and your brain will respond by trying to protect you. Your past experiences of pain shape your present response.

Experiences Rewire The Brain

If you want power over your present response, you need to have a more powerful experience to build new neural constructs and rewire the brain. You cannot undo the old constructs. Instead, you must build new ones. This process is necessary because myelin (the fiber of the brain's wiring) never unwraps. It only wraps. To rewire the painful experience in the boardroom, you need to walk into the room and see everyone enjoying cake, ice cream, and some drinks—it's party time! You need to walk into the boardroom being celebrated and hear everyone on the team show how much they appreciate that you're a part of their team. What's going to happen the next time you walk into a board meeting? You're going to be excited! You might even show up two minutes early, because a more powerful and more positive experience has helped your brain rewire itself. Pain is a part of everyone's story. Those experiences have shaped your identity up to this point. Looking back at everything that has happened can reveal clues that explain what's happening now. We can wake up, so to speak, and recognize what drives self-sabotaging behavior.

I've given you several ways of thinking about your identity, but let me give you another one: You are your mind, your psychology—how you process things. You are your brain, your neurology—the wiring of your brain. You are your physiology—your body. These three components shape your awareness of who you are. We want to develop a superior psychology and learn how we process, sequence, and frame what's happening in our lives. For these reasons, we want to learn to think through the filter of identity. We need our brain—our neurology—to rewire. How are we going to accomplish that feat? By physiologically learning to position ourselves so that we feel secure in the present moment.

This repositioning of self is essential. Let's imagine you and I are hanging out, and I pull out my phone and say, "I want to show you one of my proudest moments of anything I've ever done as a leader. I want to show you a video of me teaching my daughter how to ride a bike." Wearing the proud expression of a dad, I show you the video. You see my daughter sitting and me standing over her with a dry erase board. You watch as I verbally walk her through the four steps of riding a bike: place your foot on the pedal, swing your leg over the seat, push off, and start pedaling. I provide illustrations and diagrams. She's taking notes and filling in blanks on a worksheet. Then I ask her to put away her notes and recite the four steps of riding a bike. I'm beaming as she recites them perfectly. I say to the camera, "I taught my daughter how to ride a bike!" After a few seconds of staring at me blankly, you would tell me, "You didn't teach my daughter how to ride a bike. You only gave her the information. You don't know if she can actually ride a bike."

We have experienced so many failed attempts at change because we might have learned the content, but we never actually applied it. You can read as many leadership books as you want, but that won't actually turn you into a healthy, secure leader. First and foremost, something has to happen on the inside. Before you can order your external world, you have to order your internal world. You can't apply discipline and willpower to change who you are. The results eventually wear off. Ninety percent of people who suffer from heart disease and heart attacks don't make any changes in their lives, even after their doctors tell them they will die if they keep doing what they've been doing. Why? Because we're teaching people how to ride a bike without ever putting them on a bike.

Imagine The Experience You Need

If you want a better result and if you want to change the wiring of your brain, you have to tap into your imagination. The most powerful way to build a new baseline for your brain is to position your brain into thinking a particular experience is real. This tactic will allow you to successfully harness your imagination. You're already employing your brain to process worry and anxiety. I'm not saying you can control all the elements of anxiety, but let's learn to tap into this incredibly useful tool we have at our disposal.

This is more than visualization for your mission and community. If we could just picture ourselves winning in order to actually succeed, then Olympic athletes would win all the gold medals they want. Everyone would do it. We can use positive and negative images to momentarily affect our performance in mission and community. The imaginative experience we want to explore is geared toward forming our identity. We want to position our brain to produce a powerful rewiring experience. This space is about identity. It is not related to the results we seek for our mission and community.

This is why so many self-help resources turn me off. They leave exhausted people in their wake because they encourage us to use exaggerated and forceful visualization. You can't force yourself into a new baseline of a secure identity. You have to relax your way into it.

The greatest gift in developing who you are is the opportunity to face hardship. Going through hardship will reveal the center of your identity. All suffering is relative so it does no good to downplay your struggles by comparing them to others. If it's challenging for you, then it is meaningful and can be used for growth. When you learn what the center of your identity is, whether you have built it around something related to your mission or something related to your community, you can reframe it. You are not defined by what you do or by your relationships.

The best way to learn who you are and how to develop a secure identity is to harness the power of your imagination. I want you to learn to create an ideal space in your mind's eye or imagination. This place can be real or made up. It can be somewhere you have been or somewhere you would like to go. In your mind's eye, build this ideal space. Let your mind flip through scenes. Stop at the scene that's the most peaceful and where you feel safest; a space where you feel you don't have to prove anything. A place where fear and shame are gone. A place where you can just be. The only thing that happens here is abundance.

We have been programmed by shame. If my children are doing un-commissioned artwork on the walls and they hear me coming up the stairs, what will they do? Run and hide. Why? Because they feel shame. The shame you feel drives your reaction to either prove yourself or hide. In this space you have created, there is no feeling of shame. Most people don't know what this sensation is like. It may take some time to get there, but experiencing this reality is worth the focus. It's a place where you feel the delight of simply being you. You can learn to embrace who you are here: your interests, your hardships, the uncertainties you have about your life, and your direction. You could call this your identity space. This is what it means to rewire your brain. The process involves harnessing the power of your imagination.

Unlike the diminishing return of an addictive experience, this is a space you can go to anytime you have need and experience becoming whole after going there. I want you to focus on what it feels like, what you see, and what you hear. Earlier, we talked about recognizing lies and the moments when you feel like you have to prove yourself or hide or moments when you're frustrated and start judging those in your community. When these sensations start to occur, your capacity for leadership will be blocked. If you want to unblock it, you have to see, feel, and hear a new internal reality. What sounds do you hear? What do you see? Pay attention to these things. Typically, you will be able to do one of these actions quickly (see, feel, or hear) and the others will come with time. Go with whichever sensation is strongest for you and be satisfied with that in the beginning.

At the beginning of this book, I told you the story of how I hit rock bottom. I was struggling and barely scraping by. One day I saw a man pushing all of his belongings in a cart. Years ago I would have judged someone like that. In this instance however, I felt the vulnerability of the moment. I was a week or two away from being that guy. That fear could have energized me to go completely rigid and to prove myself or hide and give up. Instead, I was able to acknowledge that seeing this man made me feel incredibly afraid.

I was able to go somewhere internally where I'm not defined by my performance. In this internal state you learn that you're not defined by your fear. Think of all the fears we talked about in Chapter 2. This is a space where you don't feel any of those fears. In fact, you learn the opposite of fear. You can go to this space as often as you need and give yourself the gift of your identity whenever you find it necessary to do so. For me, I position myself to experience kindness, which is the opposite of my core fear, that my worth is determined by my performance.

A Few Thoughts To Help

This practice provides you with a way to hack into the benefits of mindfulness. Practice it over the course of several weeks to build a new baseline. Practice it in those urgent moments when you feel threatened and prepare for the moments you anticipate will cause you anxiety. As I was learning to train my brain to relax into a baseline of worth, I used the bathroom as a place to re-center. I know. Bring on the jokes. I would step into the bathroom when I became aware I was proving myself or hiding. I would take advantage of the change of place to relieve pressure (double entendre anyone?) and objectively look at my current state rather than be dominated by my emotions or deny them. I would use the moment of insecurity to trigger myself into becoming present in my imaginative space, the space where I was reminded that no matter what was happening externally, I was secure internally. I trained my brain. Over time you will learn to do this in the moment without having to leave the environment. Through the years, I have developed a repertoire of places. I have learned to go back through painful memories and recognize what was true and what was false. I can be present in these spaces in my mind's eye in a dynamic way. If I feel like moving or pursuing some new inspiration in these mental spaces, I do it. Sometimes I have used these spaces to connect to different parts of who I am that are still undeveloped or sequestered away. This is an idea I will develop more in the next chapter.

If you feel stuck when practicing this technique, think of the last time you remember feeling the desire that exists at the core of your fear. Go there in your mind. Go there and be present. Learn to tap into your positive memories and use them to build and develop yourself. You can gain valuable insight in this place. You can tap into a greater depth and breadth of problem solving techniques here. Don't expect the moment to always fill you with a sense of resounding truth, clarity, and purpose. Learn to simply be in the space. While in your space, allow yourself to feel, see, and hear the desire of your identity being met. Let the space teach you how to be where you are. Feel your wholeness there, whether you are experiencing good or bad circumstances in your life. Learn to give yourself permission to be yourself in this internal world, permission that you can begin to exercise in your external world. As you explore your desires and your hobbies in this place, learn to appreciate your eccentricities and your interests. Accept yourself. Give yourself permission to have whatever kind of day you're having. Nothing will block your flow like the false hype of shame and pressure. This is the space where you learn the depths of that truth. Be satisfied with doing nothing in this space. Grieve over your struggles and those moments you felt attacked for who you were if necessary. Be patient and give yourself time to allow any insights to surface. The discoveries you make in this place will allow you to address the struggles you are facing in life.

If you still feel stuck, ask yourself: "What would I do right now if I acquired an unexpected amount of time, energy, and money? Where would I go?" Go there in your mind's eye. Be there and feel no shame.

Meanwhile, learn to pay attention to how you talk to yourself. Talk to yourself about your desire for your identity. Spraying your dog's face with water because he jumped on the couch may prevent that kind of behavior in the future, but a similar practice isn't effective for your internal world. Learn to say things like, "Wow. You're really upset." Or, "Don't feel afraid. It's going to be okay." There are endless opportunities to apply this.

Make sure to enjoy the playground by the cupful rather than putting your mouth around the fire hose. We don't need you to live out the storyline of Fight Club and act like Tyler Durden.

I don't know what this space will look like for you or how you will access it. You might use imagination, meditation, or prayer. What I do know is accessing this place is the way in which you can successfully rewire your brain to start leading from an abundant mindset instead of one that is shame-based. The mind is so powerful. Highly focused athletes exercise their muscles with their minds after they have experienced an injury and require a cast. Doctors observe that when the cast is taken off, the muscle underneath hasn't atrophied.* Let's train this powerful asset.

Exercise To Complete:

1. Build your identity space. It can be real, imaginary, somewhere you have been, or somewhere you would like to go. It can be a real cabin in the woods, a picturesque beach scene you have imagined, or your childhood tree house. Like flipping through album artwork on your phone, let your mind flip through the various scenes. Receive the one that is the most peaceful and where you feel abundance, the one where you realize your fear and shame are gone.
    - Describe what it feels like, sounds like, looks like, and smells like there (Go here for the audio on learning to build a home for your identity).
    - Are you present in first person or in third person?
    - Is anyone else there with you?
    - Go there often, especially when you feel weak or threatened. This is a space where you feel secure and you know that threats to your identity are false threats. Nothing can take away from who you are.
2. Look at the fears from Chapter 2 and their corresponding desires. In your space, the desire of your identity is fully and perfectly met.

Here's an audio where I explain the below:
http://chrismcalister.podbean.com/e/no-more-proving-or-hiding/

Fears	Desires
1. If I'm not needed, then I'm not loved	Love
2. If I don't take care of myself, nobody will	Joy
3. I don't belong anywhere	Peace
4. I don't have what it takes	Patience (ability)
5. I can't perform well enough to feel worthy	Kindness (worthiness)
6. I am bad	Goodness
7. If I mess up, the worst will happen	Faithfulness (security)
8. If I'm vulnerable, I will be hurt	Gentleness (protection)
9. I am nothing special	Self-Control (uniqueness)

CHAPTER SEVEN
LOSE TO FIND

I'm bored' is a useless thing to say.
You live in a great, big, vast world that you've
seen none percent of. Even the inside of your own mind
is endless; it goes on forever, inwardly, do you
understand? The fact that you're alive is amazing.
So you don't get to be bored.

LOUIS C.K.

I woke up in excruciating pain. After standing, I immediately fell to the floor and crawled to the couch. Something was wrong. I didn't know my lower back could hurt so incredibly much. Over the years, problems with spasms had given me trouble, but this was different, and it required special attention. After receiving a number of chiropractic treatments over a few days, I could finally move. Not wanting to return to that state, I bought a book on lower back exercises. Eventually, I learned that I had been slouching and failing to engage the muscles in my lower back in order to hold my spine in a healthy position. Now, after years of performing these exercises and doing yoga, my body feels uncomfortable if I slouch my lower back. A healthy posture creates the foundation for the proper function of our bodies.

In this chapter, we will walk through the ways to posture yourself in order to experience a secure identity. When coupled with the understanding of how the brain processes experiences, you will begin to recognize with greater and greater efficiency those moments when you operate out of insecurity. You will learn the skills to quickly reframe your pain and your shame.

People use a variety of avenues to find themselves such as work, religious systems, hobbies, and relationships. A person can also become lost in these very same places. Many people attach to those places as a means to break from the relentless agony of shame that plagues their work and relationships. Eventually, they consider them the center of who they are. Recently, I watched a documentary on Richard Prior. He initially failed in pursuing a comedic career, but after making a renewed effort, found his voice. On stage he was a star, becoming the first comedian to captivate both black and white audiences, but off stage he was fighting a losing battle with cocaine addiction.

It's easy for us to succeed in our mission and feel amazing but then, like Prior, step off the stage and feel less whole. Everything around us is either forming or deforming us, and the difference between forming and deforming experiences is based on how we process what's happening. You have probably felt intense joy after establishing a connection with another human being or the adrenaline rush that accompanies a win in an important mission. Likewise, you may have also experienced what it's like to lose who you are in the midst of your mission or in your community. You might feel so amazing when you have a meaningful relationship with someone, but when you go through a breakup, you stop and wonder, "Who am I as a result of this?" Or perhaps you experience a win at work and feel amazing, only to have a big loss in the next quarter and feel a sense of despair.

If we're going to be the best leaders we can possibly be and if we're going to be engaged and empowering, we need to figure this out. We can't be crushed by loss and we can't be swept away by intense euphoria in a win. The solution isn't to reject all the joy, purpose, and fun we have with our hobbies, religion, work, and relationships. I want to experience more benefits from these areas of my life. Way more. I bet you do too. The key is in how we process or experience these facets of life. We don't want to merely experience momentary relief. We also want to learn who we are in the midst of our lives.

If you don't know who you are apart from your mission and community, then you won't be able to completely engage in your mission. Your adrenaline will blind you when you win, and you will feel absolutely crushed when you lose. In relationships, you will often feel as though the other person completes you. Unfortunately, if you happen to lose that relationship, you will feel adrift and lost. No human being can meet all the needs of your identity. No work can give you all the answers to address the fears we discussed in Chapter 2. How do you engage in your mission and community in a way that opens up more of who you are and allows you to have an experience where you learn something profound about yourself? Thinking, analyzing, worrying, stewing, and ruminating on how best to plan out your life does not add up to living. When life is tough, there's a part of your brain that is panicking. There is another part of your brain that can help calm you down. To find yourself, to find out who you are beyond your work and community, you need to find a way to calm your brain down.

Trigger Yo' Self

We need to incorporate emotional experiences that make us feel alive. (WARNING: Many use this method to justify self-sabotaging behavior. When people feel lost and are experiencing a sense of numbness, they often engage in destructive behavior and binge on the false sensation of living a meaningful life. Any activity we use to meet the needs of our identity is dangerous until we are aware of our true motives.) The practice I encourage involves creating space that allows you to develop who you are and deepens your sense of meaningful commitments, while increasing your capacity for happiness and joy.

In the last chapter, you created a space in your mind's eye. In this chapter, we want to find that space in the physical world. I want you to think about some activity where you feel peace, you feel joy, and you feel more whole simply because of partaking in that activity. This could be dinner with friends, a hike in the woods, walking your dog, playing catch with your son, cooking a meal, or developing a strategic plan to use at work. It doesn't matter what it is, but it has to be a moment where you feel alive and you're not driven by fear and shame. Once you're in that space, creatively think through the process of building a bridge out of that activity that will allow you to access the rest of your day.

Whatever this "identity activity" is, you will know you have found something that you can build upon when it opens you up to gratitude and allows you to surrender to the day. It will open up your senses and keep you from over-analyzing. If you're a novice in this activity and you find yourself becoming stressed, try something different. We want to enter it with the same eagerness of a child learning to go down a slide. For those who are more advanced, find an activity that positions you to give to others what you are afraid you lack in your own identity. Creatively open yourself up to an activity that will allow you to feel the opposite of the fear you learned about in Chapter 2. What activity helps you feel worthy simply because you are alive and not tied to your performance? What activity fills you with abundance, allowing you to be patient with yourself and later allowing you to be patient with others? What activity helps you feel that you belong regardless of the misunderstandings others might have about you? Write yourself a giant permission slip to make as much time as you can for this activity.

Later, stack physical stimuli in order to anchor this feeling. Use music, flavor, sensations of climate, and tactile awareness to anchor this new baseline or posture as deeply as possible. As I mentioned in the last chapter, I stumbled onto this enlightening practice with canoeing. Since then, I have built many triggers and routines that help me store what security in my identify feels like in my mind and body. The physical movement allows the mental wrestling to subside. There are endless applications of this practice. Let me flesh out a more robust example.

Imagine you chose cooking for your activity. Before you cook, practice going to the space in your mind's eye as discussed in Chapter 6. Be present with it, deeply so. Play a song that helps you feel an abundance of your identity that is the opposite of your fear. Now go cook. Be present. Be aware of the cilantro on the tips of your fingers. Feel the vegetables as you chop them. Take a deep belly breath and smell them. Play the song again while you are cooking. Eat. Enjoy every bite, and occasionally picture yourself in your space from the last chapter. Increase your awareness of the environment. Are there birds singing? Do you notice any clouds? Is there something that seems insignificant yet has the potential to mesmerize you completely? Increase your awareness of your body. Is there stress in your body? Increase your awareness of your internal world. Is there something to explore within you? You have the opportunity to endlessly explore your internal world. Before you clean up, play the song again to seal this moment.

If you do this often enough, you will eventually be able to hear the song and relax your way into who you truly are in the midst of meeting life's many demands. As you continue to practice this activity, you will be able to hear a few chords from the song and trigger yourself into entering this state on demand. You can use this song to help you before you enter into situations that you anticipate will be stressful or risky in some way. High level athletes often use this practice for championship games. You can use it for your daily life.

When carrying out the activity, do not approach it from a rigid standpoint. You will face distractions, but you do not have to force them away from you. Let them pass through you. The siren will pass. The surprise irritations will pass. Return to the moment.

As you repeat your activity, look for a way to incorporate a tactile reminder you can touch and hold throughout the day. If walking the dog is your activity, perhaps you could get a key chain with a dog charm and your dog's name. Maybe your activity is photography, so you put a screensaver on your phone that is related to photography or reminds you of the process of picking out your subject and capturing an image when your shutter clicks. This activity isn't about building a bridge to escape from what's happening in your mission and community. It's about being able to accelerate your life by downshifting into first gear in the midst of stressful demands and pressures. It provides an anchor, ensuring that when you have a major win you won't become hyped out of your mind and chase after a fantasy. Building this bridge also ensures that when you lose, you won't experience crushing feelings of despair and lose your momentum and ability to strategize. This activity allows you to remain steady and secure.

While this method will help you navigate the wins and losses of life, the most important need for this is in the wilderness. The moments when you feel despair or disillusioned represent moments of tremendous potential. The mountaintops don'tchange you. You learn who you really are when life doesn't seem to make sense or add up.

These moments train you to become elite in awareness. In the beginning, I might only be aware of the fact that I have punched a door or snapped at an employee. Over time, I will begin to recognize the intensity of tone. As I continue to grow in awareness, I will notice tension in my face before shaping my tone in more heated moments. Gradually, I will be able to notice my elevated heart rate and slow it down before I punch the door. The mystical among us are not gifted in a particularly special way. They simply learned how to slow down time.

Welcome Yourself

There's one more element to finding yourself, and it is for the advanced. Using the skill you developed in the last chapter, I want you to picture yourself at a table in your mind's eye. Notice all the details of the table. Make it any design or style of table you want, but make sure there is plenty of seating. Part of what you are doing in the activity is learning to bring the fullness of who you are into that activity. For example, when I get stressed, the playful part of who I am goes away. Playful Chris disappears and leader Chris powers up and becomes rigid. To counteract this occurrence, I use the table exercise to welcome all of who I am to the table. There are parts of you that are most welcome at the table. There are other parts of you that have been exiled.

Here is something incredible: You had to exile parts of who you are in order to survive intense pain in your life. Good job. You did fantastic work surviving that pain. Now the task of adulthood is to welcome back the parts of who you are that you once banished.

Welcome all of you to the table. Welcome the artistic part of who you are. Welcome the bold part who can confidently ask for what she needs. Welcome the sensitive part who is afraid of what others will think of him. During a strenuous season, I once took my kids to the pool. It had a basketball hoop in the water. The lifeguards blew their whistles for adult swim, and I got in the pool and grabbed the ball. I communicated with my body that I was taking and keeping this space from other kids so I could play with mine. The little kid in me wanted to play, and he needed to have permission to command the table for a while. The lifeguard blew the whistle, my kids jumped in the pool, and I continued to play my worries away with them.

Sometimes there are parts of you that need to show up for certain reasons. Sometimes there are parts of you that have been gone for a long time. Learn to draw on all the resources of who you are. Learn to draw on the unwelcomed parts of who you are and amplify their presence at the table as necessary. As you do this, you will find that you have often faced your problems using similar tactics throughout your life. Surprisingly, what you did in junior high to navigate a painful moment can be done again. There is much here to explore.

When Richard Prior gets on stage, there's a part of him that comes alive. Once he leaves the stage, he doesn't have access to that part anymore. He is hollowed out on the inside. In a search to find himself on stage, he lost himself in life.

You don't have to stop being a leader to figure out who you are. You don't have to remove all the pressure. There will always be some level of pressure. You can recover on the run and in the midst of pressure by learning to position yourself to have new experiences. If you commit to this activity and the table exercise, then you will find yourself.

Exercises to Apply:

1. Find an activity, physical space, environment, or anything that opens you up and helps you feel secure. (In the last chapter we talked about brain, mind, and body. This part of positioning yourself refers to the body.) It could be dinner with friends, a hike in the woods, walking your dog, playing catch with your son, cooking a meal, or ______________________. We are looking for a space where you forget about the needs of your identity and don't feel shame. In this space, you feel relaxed. You feel free.

2. Learn to partake in that activity in a small way throughout your day. Stacking micro moments throughout your day is what changes your brain's wiring. So if you find walking your dog to be an incredibly joyful experience, then get a keychain with your breed of dog on it or your dog's name. Reach into your pocket and touch the keychain whenever you feel falsely threatened in your identity throughout the day. After

connecting this with the experience of walking your dog, you will be able to tap into this emotional state anytime you need to. There are endless ways to apply this practice. Get creative.

3. Do this powerful table exercise. Think about all the parts that compose who you are. Sit at a table in your mind and welcome all the parts of who you are to the table. For me, there's goofy Chris, strategic Chris, angry Chris, etc. There are certain parts of you that have been banished from the table. Welcome them back. Initially, their banishment helped you survive, but now welcoming them back will help you thrive. Reflect on how the active space from the first exercise most effectively nurtures the parts of you that need to grow.

CHAPTER EIGHT

GIVE WHERE IT HURTS

The opposite of a fact is falsehood,
but the opposite of one profound truth
may very well be another profound truth.
NIELS BOHR

Insecurity in our identity holds us back from carrying out our mission. When we are feeling insecure, we believe we are victims of our circumstances. It's dangerous to live from insecurity. I have heard that the number one regret of hospice patients nearing the end of their lives is that they lived the life they felt pressured to live.

It's important to determine what your desires are in order to avoid this situation. Imagine my kids, old enough to work, asking my advice on whether they should apply for a job at the mall or the Apple store. At first, I would be tempted to advise them to work at the place where I can get the best discount, but ultimately, I want them to discover what they want to do. I will be careful not to express my will or place pressure on them. I want them to learn how to recognize their own desires.

What Or Who Is Driving You?

Most people have never considered the force that drives them to do the work they do or weighed the difference between true desires and false desires. Most live propped up by a lie. They read books and articles on managing stress when all the while it is actually unseen pressures that suffocate the joy out of their work. They chose a career path to keep Mom off their back, to impress someone else, or to feel closer to Dad.

You don't want to reach the end of your life and feel like you have left something un-attempted or unlived. You don't want to regret not having done something. Don't spend your life pursuing something that isn't true to who you are. Let's find clarity in what you are going after and why. Strangely enough, finding clarity begins with a contradiction of two realities:

Reality #1: Your fear reveals the area you need to focus. Your fear can help you.

Reality #2: Your fear causes you to prove yourself or hide and blocks the overflow of your brilliance in mission. Your fear can hurt you.

While opposite in nature, these realities create an incredible tension and energy that you can utilize to determine your desires. If you want to figure out what you're supposed to do, first look at what makes you afraid. Then move forward once you feel secure in your identity. The place where you feel afraid is where you will be able to most powerfully give meaning to the world.

You will either do your work from an insecure identity or from a secure identity. If you do it from an insecure identity, you seek to get. If you do it from a secure identity, on the other hand, you seek to give. When I move into my mission from a healthy place, it's better both for me and for the people I help. I overflow. What are you trying to get or give? Whatever your fear is, it must be answered. If your fear is that you're not worthy unless you perform well, you will try to celebrate your worth through performance.

If you fear you don't have a place where you belong, you will try to find belonging in your work. The insecurity and neediness with which you move through that space is going to push people away, and you won't be able to fulfill your desires or help others grow.

How do you change that? How do you give worth to others through your work? How do you bring a sense of belonging to others in your work? You flip it. Nothing will block your ability to follow clear and healthy direction in your work like doing it from an insecure identity. And the opposite is true. Nothing will reveal clarity in your mission like having a profound sense of security. You give what you have not been given.

You Become Unstoppable

When you learn who you are, that clarity is going to overflow into action. You will have to try that thing, whatever your thing happens to be. You can't help but do it. It may still be hard. Sometimes really hard. It's still work, after all, but it is thrilling and enjoyable work. When your work comes out of a secure identity, it no longer defines your life. In fact, you learn to live from overflow, which transcends your job. This isn't about the nine-to-five, it's about all that we do. Use the trigger you learned in the last chapter to frame all your actions as an opportunity to give, regardless of your fear. This practice changes how you move in and out of those spaces you typically occupy. You bring a secure and focused "doing" into all your roles, commitments, and performances.

I want to help you live with a clear mission. To get there, having a security identity is crucial. That's where we started. Now that you have the framework for creating a secure identity, let's zero in on your mission. And if you're at Chapter 8 of this book, you know this by now: we start with the pain.

There's a difference between identity pain and mission pain. Identity pain occurs when negative events happen and shame transforms them into a lie about who you are. Mission pain occurs when the deal falls through, you don't get the job, or someone feels let down by your performance. If you can learn to separate identity pain from mission pain, you can learn to be resilient. Grit or resilience is a greater indicator of success than your intelligence. And fortunately, resilience can be learned. This is why I celebrate the identity of those around me and praise their effort.

There are no guarantees as to how your mission will play out, but as long as you are not defined by the results (whatever they may be) you can keep going no matter what. Everything that happens in your mission becomes an opportunity to grow and develop your skills while simultaneously deepening your awareness of your identity. When your plan fails, revisit the identity space. Repeat the identity activity. Position yourself to experience a secure identity. Then you will be able to keep going regardless of what happens. You can unblock innovation because your mission won't be energized from a place of proving yourself or hiding.

It's Called Vulnerability For A Reason

If you want to be a leader who energizes, you will have to lead with vulnerability. That might sound counterintuitive, but ambitious people who pretend to have it all together keep their team in a tense and uptight state. Entrepreneurs and leaders who express appropriate vulnerability relax their team, allowing them to perform better. We all know nobody has it all together, so we can stop pretending. Leaders who aren't vulnerable are trying to prove something or hide themselves, and everyone in the room can tell. Insecure leaders drain their team. Vulnerable leaders energize their team.

How are you vulnerable? Be human with those around you. It doesn't mean you need to have a breakdown or be excessively needy. Be present in the moment with them. Whatever you do, whether you're delivering a vision or navigating a conflict, engage with nothing to prove, nothing to hide. It's beautiful, it's fun, and it gets results. The quickest way to energize yourself for mission is to give in those areas where you have been hurt. You give where you have not been given.

The thing that keeps us from being present and human in those moments is a fear of being hurt. As a leader, you will be hurt. When you build who you are around a secure identity and are not defined by your mission or your community then you're free of what others think of you. You can be engaged and vulnerable. Share the places where you don't have it all together or don't have all the answers. Let your team be great where they are great. The higher you go in your leadership, the more you will trust the people around you to do what needs to be done. Only a healthy, secure leader doesn't feel the need to be the smartest person in the room. As a leader, I would rather focus on being the most aware.

One night, I was typing up an email to clients in a coaching cohort and I left my computer open while I went to the kitchen. While I was away from my computer my nine-year-old daughter sat down and typed something that she thought was only to me and referenced our Nerf gun war. She typed, "I will kill you tonight." That line was buried in the email without my knowledge. Two clients replied, alerting me to the hidden message. A decade ago, that would have really bothered me. I would have been consumed by how it might have made me look unprofessional. But through everything I am sharing with you in this book, I have learned to relax. This time, I gave her a high five! I was able to enjoy the hilarity of the moment. I want you to think of a situation in the past week where you were disappointed with work. What's something you wanted but work failed to deliver? Whatever it was, flip it. This week, think of one area where you can give someone what you felt like you missed out on. How can you move from grasping to giving? The feeling of missing out is a false perception. Everything you want is connected to your identity, and it is already yours. That's why we have to train the brain. Learning to work from a giving mindset shapes you to lead with engagement. It rewires your brain to lead from abundance.

A Tool To Provoke

To explore more clearly what it means for you to give where it hurts, draw a Venn diagram. Circle one is play, which could be components reminiscent of your childhood or what excites you now. Circle two is pain, which is your fear and hurt. Circle three is called magic. It's making the tricky stuff you do look easy.

There was stuff you did as a kid that was play to you. But we still play as adults. Play takes place when you lose your concern about the management of your career's trajectory or how you look to others. Examine those things in the diagram to find a way to build a bridge to that state of mind in your life now. I started a business in ninth grade making and selling necklaces. For me to leverage my skills, time, and energy away from the non-profit sector and into the business sector was a natural progression.

In circle two, ask, "Where have I been hurt?" You will give most powerfully to the world in your mission in the places you are afraid and have been hurt. I was hurt by organizations that put corporate vision before the development of the individual. They wanted to get to the bottom line, and it didn't matter if the people were growing and developing in leadership or not. For me, there was pain there. Now I love helping entrepreneurs, artists, and ambitious people lead out of security, empowering them to have a major effect on the whole of culture.

Then the circle I call magic. It's the thing you do that doesn't come so naturally to other people. They may not know how much effort you applied to develop and grow that skill, but it's something you do that is marked by a sense of overflow. It's the thing you do well, and you make it look easy. Draw these circles out: play, pain, and magic. Draw your diagram and spend some time thinking about what this looks like for you. Not all alignment with regards to your mission is a lightning strike or something that happens quickly. Instead, it's 10,000 steps in the direction you want to go. It's a gradual unfolding. I have spent time in work that was play and magic but wasn't aligned with pain. Then I did work that was a combination of pain and magic, but not play. The more you put into this journey, the more time you spend thinking through this concept, the more you will gain clarity on your path. This is a tool to provoke thinking, not provide easy answers.

Too many people live in the extremes of one of these circles. Those that carry out their mission only from the pain circle become martyrs. Because they are living out of pain, they are willing to ruin themselves for the mission. Those that only pursue their mission from the magic circle put on a show for others but lack the substance they desire to convey. Those that only do mission from the play circle run from the gravitas they could live with because it's easier to hide behind playing at life.

When considering these different areas of the diagram, be careful not to stereotype jobs. You might assume comedians only do their mission from the play circle because they are jokers. Yet what makes good comedy brilliant is the exposure of truth. You might assume those in non-profits are seeking to change the world with a martyr's mindset, yet their ease and playfulness attract donors who take everything too seriously. Resist the urge to judge and stereotype. Study your own expression of mission instead.

Go Back To The Table

As you assess your own expression of mission, there is one more critical area to give where it hurts. Relational conflict or discord will block the expression of your mission. Not paying attention to this area will distract you internally and cause you to waste a lot of energy moving sideways rather than moving forward.

Think of someone with whom you are having a conflict. It might be someone you are mad at, someone you don't see often, or a partner in business or love. It might be someone you don't know personally but feel angst toward. It could even be the invisible "they" that you often feel pressured by. Now revisit the table exercise from the previous chapter. In your mind's eye, invite that person to your table and tell them what you want them to give you. For instance: "I want you to celebrate me and make me feel worthy." Then apologize to them. Tell them, "I made you responsible for giving me worth and I release you from that." Repeat this exercise as necessary. Write it out if you need to. Keep yourself unblocked. Use this strategy when you become aware of the conflict. Use this strategy to prepare for upcoming conversations that might be tense. This will keep you from engaging in those conversations with your word gun cocked and ready to fire. When something like that happens, it screams insecurity. You make someone else responsible for the needs of your identity. It's normal to get blocked by relational hurt and confusion. The key to preventing it is efficiently organizing and processing that confusion.

After reading this chapter, you might feel compelled to make some kind of change. But before you make one, you need to be able to reframe all of your doing through this identity filter. You may eventually change your job to better align with your identity, but first gain clarity on the narrative fear and shame have created in your life. When you downshift into first gear you will put yourself on the path to fulfilling your mission from a healthy core. This is overflow. Then at the end you will have lived your life, not the one you felt pressured to live.

Exercises To Complete:

1. Find a situation in the past week where you were disappointed with work. What did it fail to give you that you wanted? How can you complete a task today or this week and give to someone that thing you feel like you missed out on? The feeling of missing out is a false perception as you already have everything you need in your identity. Learning to work from a giving mindset shapes you to lead with engagement and re-wires your brain to lead from abundance. If you are a business owner and want a more advanced application, examine the feel of your business culture and the system of messaging. Shape the culture and messaging around what you can give.

2. Nail down your guiding vision for your mission. Draw three overlapping circles (a Venn diagram). Label the circles 1. Play (childhood) 2. Pain (fear/hurt) 3. Magic (Easy). There are no overnight solutions or easy answers here. When folks have questions about their work, I often ask them to show me where they would place their work in these circles. The point is to be honest about their place and what they can experiment with in order to get in the overlapping sweet spot of the three circles. Plot yourself. What actions could you take to move towards one of the other circles that isn't represented by your work? Figuring out your passion and following it have become too complicated. Find the next step towards your desire and take it.

3. It's normal to get blocked up relationally with instances of hurt or confusion. The differentiator is how quickly you can organize and process the confusion. Think of someone you are in conflict with. In your mind's eye, invite them to the table you envisioned in the last chapter. Tell them what you want them to give you. Word it in such a way that it is accurate and based on your fear. Example: "I want you to

celebrate me and make me feel worthy." Then tell them, "I apologize to you. I made you responsible for providing me with _______________ . I release you from that." Any actual conversation that takes place with them after this exchange is a bonus. Maybe you need to define a boundary with them or lay out some parameters of business. Use this as necessary.

CHAPTER NINE

IMPROVE DECISION MAKING

The worst thing you do when you think is lie — you can make up reasons that are not true for the things that you did....

RAY BRADBURY

Making decisions can induce anxiety. Not only do we need to be aware that we can deceive ourselves, we also need to be aware that we are suffering from decision fatigue. For the ambitious, for the creative, for the entrepreneur and for the leader, multiple decisions need to be made on a daily basis. I will drive my car with a nail in the tire, stopping at gas stations along the way to put air in it because I don't have extra energy to solve that problem. Developing a healthy approach to decision making helps to protect against deceiving yourself and fights off decision fatigue. Ultimately, it helps you make brilliant decisions quickly.

The starting point for solid decision making is to discover the motives behind your decisions. I can't properly navigate this process and make good decisions when I make those decisions from a need to get something from my mission or community. In contrast, I think more clearly when I allow my identity to overflow into my mission or my community.

The difference between panicked decisions or purposeful decisions comes down to our motives. What are you trying to get from the decision? What's the reward you're seeking? If I try to find validation, meaning, acceptance, home, belonging, safety, worth, or any other desire from my mission or my community, I am setting myself up to make a bad decision. As I break this down for you, I need to show you how the fears we talked about in Chapter 2 apply to decision making. Then we will develop an approach to protect you as you move forward.

Fear 1: If I'm Not Needed, I'm Not Loved

If you make decisions from this fear, you react in a way that pleases others. You will make decisions to ensure people like you. This is going to hurt your leadership. Everyone wants to be liked, but if the filter you're using to make a decision is to make others like you, then you will avoid making the hard calls that will move the organization forward.

This fear also shows up in significant relationships. You're not able to have healthy boundaries because you're always reacting in a way that makes them happy with you. You will not make great relationship decisions when fear is driving you.

Fear 2: If I Don't Take Care Of Myself, No One Else Will

You will share your despair about the present moment to test others and their commitment to you when this fear drives your decision making. Author Brene Brown calls it "spotlighting" when you are too vulnerable too quickly and give too much information.

I have seen this happen in relationships. I have seen it happen in leadership. You will make bad decisions about how vulnerable you should be because you will test others' commitment to you. Sometimes it isn't just over sharing about your personal life. When you constantly require those you lead to match your intensity, you're testing their commitment. You fail to understand two realities: 1) More intensity won't solve the problem. You need clarity. 2) Not all personalities are the same. Someone else could be passionate, but not express it like you do. If you struggle with this fear, you will wear out the people around you. Your key leaders won't stay very long.

Fear 3: I Don't Belong Anywhere

If you make decisions from this fear, you will ignore present discomfort and problems. When you have that difficult or dreaded family conversation, you won't want to deal with the reality. You want to kick the can further down the road. When you're in a meeting, you will ignore unpleasant data or the obvious chaos that needs to be addressed because you want to keep everybody happy. It's a false sense of peace. You want to feel like you belong, so you never solve the problem that needs to be solved. The desire to find a place to belong will keep you from solving problems that need definitive solutions. The fear of being excluded or disliked will block your ability to become a great leader.

Fear 4: I Don't Have What It Takes

This fear will be exposed if you are afraid to try something new, or if you go to the other extreme and brashly jump in without investigating. At work, this fear is evident if you won't volunteer for the new thing because you're afraid of being exposed as inadequate. It's easy to identify if you will blindly accept a new assignment without taking into account whether or not you possess the skills required and enough time to accomplish it.

Fear 5: I Can't Perform Well Enough To Feel Worthy

You will ignore present concerns in favor of chasing an ideal future if this fear drives your decisions. You will be driven to achieve great accomplishments and dream about your future goals because you falsely believe worth and performance are connected.

There is value in having a vision for the future, but this is a horrible way of leading. You are burning people out and dragging them along with you. They may not have the same capacity or drive, but it doesn't mean they are ineffective. Your frustration with them might stem from the fact that deep down you are fried and resent that they are more honest and centered. I once participated in an exercise at a leadership training that divided our group into teams and immersed us into stressful situations. We were in a wooded area and two people fell down pretending to be injured. Our team had two hours to build a stretcher for our two "injured" people and move them to the "helicopter pad." I was the leader and I started delegating. I systematized our process. The team was operating at an awesome level. We made the stretcher and carried our "injured" people out. The event organizers told us it was the best stretcher any team had ever built. I felt amazing until in the debriefing one of the ladies in our group said, "You got the job done, but you burned me out doing it."

That statement accurately sums up the worst side of my leadership when I'm under intense pressure and ignore my fears. I'm going to make bad decisions when I strive towards the future. I will burn out my team, and it will deform me. Everything you're doing either makes you a better version of yourself or a worse one. When I lead for the future and cover up present concerns, I don't pay attention to what's happening inside me. I am deformed.

Fear 6: I Am A Bad Person

When this is your fear, you will hype yourself into making a change by trying to force new habits, but they always fade. You're a good starter. You can drum up that initial momentum. Unfortunately, you are not good at the middle or the end when the momentum fades. You start out with rabbit intensity, and then you fizzle out because you tried to fool yourself into being different. It comes back to believing deep down that you're a bad person. It's self-sabotaging behavior. You dive into the new job with bravado and zeal. Then after you make a mistake, you self-talk your way into a further spiral. You falsely believe that your suspicions about who you are were confirmed. Or you jump into the relationship riding high on the chemical cocktail of attraction. When you hurt the other person you believe all your relationships fall apart because you are broken.

Fear 7: If I Mess Up, The Worst Will Happen

If you make decisions through the filter of this fear, you will cling to nostalgia from a moment or season in your past when you felt safe. If you're always drifting to the past with your relationships, it's because you feel scared and uncertain about the future so you will go back to what you know. If you lead a staff meeting with this fear, you don't inspire them to change or blaze off into the future. You recount past accomplishments. This will block your ability to have great relationships and become a leader who leads at the highest level because you have to make peace with the fact that there is no certainty in mission or community. The only certainty is in your identity. You can know who you are. That can be defined and secure. A secure identity provides stability even if everything within your mission and community changes.

Fear 8: If I'm Vulnerable, I'll Be Hurt

If this is your fear, you try to keep people bought in so they don't leave. Rather than leading with full engagement, you're so scared they will leave that you constantly build walls to shut them out. Those closest to you in relationships always feel at an arm's distance even if you falsely think they are close. You will even drum up artificial conflict to push people away because you're afraid. The conflict doesn't feel artificial in the moment however, it can be easy to see situations that were blown out of proportion or used to escalate a situation to a desired reaction. You, as a leader, create a wake of chaos and conflict.

Fear 9: I'm Nothing Special

When you believe you're nothing special, you will make decisions to stay in small ponds. You will be afraid to expose yourself by choosing jobs or objectives that will take you to the edge of your abilities. You will complain about being lonely but not take steps to foster relationships with people different from you. Continuing to shrink back from taking risks and trying new things will keep you from critical pivots and momentum in business. It will keep you stuck relationally. You will constantly get in your own way.

Making Better Decisions

Once you are aware of the fear you can begin to think about decision making like a train track with two parallel rails. The first rail represents the need for you to face reality and the second represents how your decisions can teach you about your identity.

The first rail of making a decision from a secure identity is to face reality. You will never have enough information or clarity to guarantee the results of your decisions. Four questions that will help you honestly face reality:

1. Am I distorting reality to force the story I want to be true? We have a tendency to talk ourselves into what isn't real because our brain is forcing a false narrative. Out of fear and insecurity we force the story we want to be true and distort reality. Until we are secure in who we are and don't need the results from our mission or something from our community to fill that hole, we are unable to face reality. When I was recovering from a major financial mistake, I reminded myself throughout the day, "Chris, you have six figures of debt." I wasn't trying to beat myself up about it. I was trying to face the reality of it.

2. Am I looking for one fact to justify what I feel and cover up concerns? This is why you buy things, both big and small. You may buy a house even if it stretches your budget because you feel a strong emotion. You allow that strong emotion to override facts and figures to justify the financial commitment, deluding yourself that it will work out somehow. If you are secure in who you are, you don't need to have that house or drive that car to feel whole. You don't have to look for one fact to justify what you feel and cover up your concerns. Instead, you pay attention to the concerns.

3. Am I counting on external factors I can't control and chasing a fantasy? Most people get distracted because they are chasing a fantasy. Philosopher Nassim Nicholas Taleb talks about using 20 percent of your resources for risky bets while focusing 80 percent on what you know moves it forward. Stop making your decisions based on external factors that are out of your control. Focus on what you know moves it forward. There will be moments to take a risk and try crazy things. Some will work and some might fail. Regardless of the outcome, keep your eyes open in those long shots to see how to approach it again next time so you can learn from the hits and misses.

4. Am I aware of the primary reason I could hijack my decision making? Most people aren't. Gut-check yourself with this question. If your fear is that you're not worthy unless you perform well, you will make a decision to try to get more worth. You will hijack your decisions. The

primary reason you would hijack your decision making is because your fear blinds you.

The second rail of the decision-making train track is learning who you are in the mistakes. It's easier to learn who you are after a mistake than a success. As you process your mistakes, understand that you will never eliminate all the mistakes. This isn't about regret or shame. This is about learning and evaluating. You catch glimpses of who you are when you mess up. Mistakes do not define you. They simply uncover insight into why you made that poor decision.

When you do make mistakes you can learn to eliminate making the same ones and use the current ones to your advantage. World class performers focus on eliminating mistakes in stressful situations and leveraging any mistakes made for propulsion. Superior athletes know how to reattach to the present moment. If Michael Jordan misses three jump shots in a row he doesn't go to the bench fighting a mental game. He steps back on the court in the present moment, not internally distracted or beating himself up. He doesn't lose the ability to recover the mental game and enter back into flow. Think of a poor decision you made in the past. The point of this exercise is not to shame you. The ability to analyze a poor decision is essential in learning how to separate who you are from what you have done. Feeling secure in the present means you can evaluate past decisions without being defensive. So think about this decision, and ask yourself, "Why did I make that decision?"

Be Your Own Sage

You get to be your own sage. Look at the way you're making decisions and how your core fear can botch those up. Imagine someone telling you a story that helps you receive insight into your fears and who you are.
I know my story, and I know what I need to hear. There was a man who needed a house for his family. They were cold and hungry. He quickly threw together a home. He skipped the unseen and most expensive part of the house: the foundation. Hurriedly, he built the wall. Skipping the insulation, he hung the drywall. He put up beautiful crown molding. Then he welcomed his family into the home. After a few weeks, the flooring sagged. Walls began to sink and warp. He ignored reality and the inevitable danger as he kept promising something better in the future. The house caved in.

This is the story I remind myself of when making decisions. I gut-check by asking, "Am I covering up any concerns?" Often I will catch myself texting and making an on-the-spot decision. Instead of responding before I've had time to analyze any concerns that I might be covering up, I've learned to quickly, almost reflexively, ask this question. For bigger decisions I move slower. Even if I want to respond immediately, I intentionally make myself wait before I respond. I often still move forward even when there are concerns. I can't wait until everything is perfect, but by acknowledging the concerns, I can build the best possible foundation.

Your story can also help you assess which type of decision maker you are. Some wait too long. Some jump too soon. Learn which one is your dominant style. If you jump too soon then take your time. If you wait too long, learn to approach your decisions from the reality that the only certainty you can have is in your identity. You will never be guaranteed how your decisions will effect your mission and community. If you forget this, the volatility of life will cause you stress. You will rigidly resort back to your worst decision-making patterns.

Get creative. What story would someone tell you? Write it out or record it in audio form. You have your identity space and identity activity. Now find your identity story. It can be as simple or embellished as you need. Dive into this to improve your decision making and hone your ability to make decisions from a secure identity. Don't make bad decisions from fear. Instead, make great choices now that you know abundance.

No Forced Solutions

We have covered the why and the what. Now, let's determine the how. How are you going about making your decisions? Are you rushed, worried, panicked, serene, withdrawn, or engaged? Something is happening beneath the surface. Exploring the fears and writing your story will help you gain insight into what emotion might be sabotaging your decisions..

Part of understanding how you make decisions is learning to avoid the extremes of putting off decisions and deciding to decide. You can't solve all of your problems immediately and ignoring them won't make them go away. Let me share a visual example of how I acknowledge problems in and around me. I picture myself looking out over a horizon. I see 1-3 big problems, 5-7 medium problems, and 10-13 small problems. This is my personal capacity for holding problems in my mental cache. Your personal capacity may initially be less than mine. Instead of being overwhelmed with 3-20 problems you are facing, use this visual metaphor to symbolize this reality: you don't have to be threatened by the presence of problems. Address and solve the issues that are urgent. Be willing to wait weeks or months for other possible solutions to present themselves. Sometimes a problem might require several different attempts before you have a resolution. Challenge yourself to have multiple solutions ready. I started this very book that way. There were questions regarding how I was going to fund certain elements. I moved forward while still paying attention to the concerns. I tried multiple ways to get funding. Eventually, one worked. If you could solve every problem on your horizon, you would have all new problems. Anxiously forcing a solution moves you backward.

Why So Serious?

Before this chapter on improving your decision making comes to end, I want you to notice how you engage the moments you relax or reward yourself. When you get too serious, you lose the ability to play and access all of who you are. Pay attention to the underlying "how" in the decisions you make in those moments when you need to give yourself rest, reprieve, and renewal. These are the decisions that aren't necessarily the best for you, but in certain moments, are the right things for you.

Think of it this way: No one would rationally argue that ice cream is a healthy food choice or a daily requirement. Knowing this, there are times when slowing down to enjoy a bowl of your favorite ice cream is a better choice than pushing through a project when you feel completely overwhelmed and stressed. The key is to pay attention to "how" you eat the ice cream.

Here are three mindsets you can have while you eat the ice cream. Which one is your default "how"? The first is a condemning how. You eat ice cream with an overwhelming sense of shame. You only eat the ice cream when no one is watching. You hear, "I suck. I shouldn't be eating this." The second "how" is numbing. You mindlessly eat the entire pint straight out of the container while watching your favorite TV show. The only time you notice the ice cream is when the container is empty. The third "how" is enjoyment. Be fully present when you take a walk, watch your favorite TV show, play with your dog, call a friend or eat ice cream. When you eat the ice cream with the "how" of acceptance, you enjoy each bite and soak up the endorphins. When in doubt ask, "Why so serious?"

Exercises To Complete:

1. Use this filter for checking to make sure your decisions are based on a secure identity.
    - Am I distorting reality to force the story I want to be true?
    - Am I looking for one fact to justify what I feel and covering up concerns?
    - Am I counting on external factors I can't control and chasing a

fantasy?
- Am I aware of the primary reason I could hijack my decision making?

2. Using the filter above, imagine someone approaches you with a story, correcting you mid-course to prevent a bad decision. Some make the story more visceral by writing it out. Some find a lot of clarity in making it a children's story. Be your own sage. Write your parable, your "identity story". Can you see/feel/hear the insight and clarity you now have? Move forward with this approach. Is there a current decision or track you're on that needs to change right now because of this new insight?

3. Notice "how" you're going about your decisions. Rushed? Worried? Panicked? Serene? Withdrawn? Engaged? Can you solve the urgent problems and not feel threatened by the presence of other problems?

4. How do you eat ice cream?

CHAPTER TEN MASTER CONFLICT

We constantly construct and reconstruct ourselves to meet the needs of the situations we encounter

JEROME BRUNER

When I was in high school, I drove like an idiot. Speeding tickets. Wrecks. One day I was driving 45 miles per hour in a 25 zone and I passed a police officer. His lights flicked on and fear took over. For me, in that moment, the fear wasn't of the police officer. Like most teenagers, my underlying fear was the reaction of my dad and what was going to happen to me. The fear of punishment at home drove me to make a really, really dumb decision. I slammed the gas, and instead of turning left to go home, I turned right trying to evade the police officer. It seemed rational that his outfitted cruiser was no match for my white Honda civic. I could shift gears like a pro now. I remember seeing his car with flashing lights speeding up in my rearview mirror. He pulled me over in a bank parking lot. He got out of his car and screamed, "Are you on drugs!?" He looked at the address on my driver's license, and I had to explain why I turned right instead of left. I lied, claiming that I remembered my mom asked me to buy milk. He wrote me a ticket for speeding and fleeing, followed me to the store and watched me buy milk. I went to court, stood before the judge and plead guilty to speeding but not fleeing. The teenage lawyer in me argued, "Why would I be here if I wasn't telling the truth?" The fleeing charge was thrown out. I considered applying for law school the next day.

I went through all that trouble because I feared a reaction. Conflict creates problems because we fear a reaction from others. There are couples that have been married for years that are navigating around their fears, building walls, and going to bed lonely. Businesses with a revolving door of talent are pushing people away because they fail to master conflict.

Mastering conflict is internal before it's external. All suffering, including conflict, reveals the center of our identity. We feel vulnerable in conflict, it makes us insecure and it surfaces our fears. Those fears regarding our identity drive our interactions. If we build who we are on the unstable ground of mission and community, then we will repeat self-sabotaging choices in conflict.

All conflict is a result of us trying to get someone else to meet the needs of our identity. We falsely believe we have to fight for our dignity and worth. Anger rages in the form of active anger when we feel like we have to prove our worth and take from someone else what we think we need. Or anger flares in the form of passive anger when we hide and punish others by withdrawing.

Unless we're angry in defense of a violation of who we are or we're protecting others, the anger in our life is a surface emotion. Underneath anger is fear; the fear we won't get what our identity needs, craves, and desires.

Another human being can't give us enough love, joy, belonging, safety, or any other desire to make us whole. We need to learn to live from a secure identity regardless of the state of our community or relationships then we will master conflict. We aren't blinded in the moment by what's happening. I have seen this in teams, in the boardroom, in the home, and in relationships. When we learn the four skills in this chapter, it can deconstruct any conflict, pivot the energy, and open up a beautiful space for connection.

Assess Without Attacking

To master conflict, you need to learn to assess without attacking. If you and I are fighting, I have to get out of my own way to help you get out of your own way. I have to recognize my insecurity before I can recognize yours. This takes time to learn. If I can't understand what's happening inside me, I can't understand what's happening inside you. And because I'm not aware of the fear driving my interaction, I will blindly attack you.

I was in a meeting and became very frustrated with the senior leader. There was a lack of presence, energy, and vision. As the senior leader was emotionally checking out, the glaring problem for our organization was a lack of vision. During the meeting, I was called out for a bad decision—rightly so. I had made a mistake. But instead of paying attention to what I needed to learn from that, I passed the blame. I blurted out, "The problem here is the lack of vision." I attacked in defensiveness. This happens in every workplace, whether there are five employees or 5,000. Insecurities are firing off each other. The team leader communicates a new initiative from the senior leadership team. A mid-level manager has work that will now be wasted. She pushes against the change and the team leader feels threatened in their ability to get buy-in for the change. Two people with insecurities are ready to resist each other and it has nothing to do with the organizational direction.

Not only will we blindly attack but a lack of awareness can cause us to blindly favor others. Not understanding why we are drawn to different people leads to bad promotions and bad role changes. Certain qualities in others resonate with us because of our own insecurities. If we're not aware, we will resent people around us because they remind us of our weakness. The same attacking and favoring happens in relationships. It's why a parent often will feel an affinity towards one child and have a harder time getting along with another child. No matter how much they deny it, insecure parents play favorites. Even though parents would ideally love each child equally, it is not uncommon to feel drawn to one child more than another. It's also natural to have a child who reminds you of your weakness and triggers insecurities regularly. Most parents aren't even aware of this. They will unknowingly distance themselves from or be harsher with that child because deep down they want distance from their insecurities. Conversely, parents are often more lenient with the child who reminds them of their spouse. How the parent treats each of the children is a clue to how they treat themselves. Are they patient with mistakes or harsh? Are they kind or demanding? Are they vulnerable or powering up? Are they loving with proper boundaries or do they pressure the child to respond in certain ways so they can feel whole?

When you can assess without attacking, differences can create a stronger bond rather than a deeper separation. I know the differences between my wife and I will grow me. I learn to see the irritation in my relationship to my child as an invitation to expand. I see that uniquely wired team members are an advantage rather than an obstacle.

It took time for me to remember in the moment how my own fears escalated conflict. I would ask myself what was going on. Maybe we had a breakdown in communication and there were some sharp words exchanged in the team meeting. Healthy teams express vulnerability by not hiding or powering up in conversations but instead engage matters openly. Yet while I was learning this I would have to leave the argument and ask myself what was happening. Then it would hit me that I was attacking without assessing and interacting out of fear. Their fear fired off my fear, so I attacked.

It will take time to learn to recognize in the moment how your fears escalate conflict. You will leave an encounter and wonder how things devolved into attacking. As you become more aware of your insecurity you will learn to disarm the conflict in the moment by confessing your fear. "I'm sorry. I was scared that I looked like I didn't have it all together because this plan didn't turn out like I wanted it to." This is what it means to lead with vulnerability.

This may feel risky to you, and I understand not every place is safe. You have to learn how to navigate that in a healthy way. We'll talk more about this in the next chapter. For now, let me say that when you can call out your own problems as the team leader, you begin to set the pace for the team. When you call yourself out as the organizational leader, you have the opportunity to set a culture that flows from the top down. It takes time, but it does happen. You can do the same thing with the relationships that you value and the commitments you have.

As you become more aware, you will begin to anticipate when the people you lead will feel afraid or threatened. You will see the trouble coming and prepare to assess without attacking. You will receive what you need from your own secure identity and be able to give your team or family exactly what they need to calm their fears.

Others can't provide the abundant supply you need for your identity and you can't control the behavior of others. When you make someone else responsible for the needs of your identity, you will either try to manipulate them or pull away from the relationship. You can't manipulate, control, or punish someone enough to fix your insecurity. Tearing down others or withholding love won't move you from scarcity to abundance. You get that internally in your identity space. Then you can assess without attacking.

Ask For What You Need

The second way you master conflict is to ask for what you need. This isn't complicated. It's as simple as saying, "I need this from you." I see this play out in my marriage. During a conversation about a poor financial decision we made, my wife literally used the word "we" as the decision was one we both had agreed on, but I heard her say "you." I felt myself become insecure and defensive. I was learning to downshift during insecure moments, so I was able to calm down in the moment, recognize she is not responsible for the needs of my identity, and ask for clarity. I said to her, "When you say 'we,' I'm hearing 'you.' Can I ask for insight on that? Do you mean this is something we've done together, or do you think I'm responsible for this?" One of my business partners, who helps keep me sane and focused, had a habit of routinely joking with me: "If SightShift gets weird and fluffy and gross, I'm out." It always bugged me a bit and finally, I took my own advice and asked for what I needed. I said, "When you say that, all I hear is, 'I'm thinking about leaving.'" When we can speak our truth vulnerably to others, it opens the door for a deeper relationship. My partner stopped throwing around jokes about quitting because he knows it triggered me.

When two people are communicating without awareness they will hear what is being said through the filter of their own fear. "Why haven't you taken out the trash?" can turn into, "I wish you weren't here." One is spoken. The other heard. I will often ask the person I'm communicating with to respond back in their own words what they heard me say. I want to know if I need more insight on how to communicate to them.

Sometimes asking for what you need isn't about insight. It's about asking for a practical response that's going to help you feel differently. You can use this at work: "I've been working a ton of hours and I feel like that isn't being remembered." That's not an accusatory statement. "I need to talk about aligning my responsibilities with my skills." Or, "I need to talk about reorganizing my weekly flow and calendar." Your situation is unique. You know how safe the people around you might be. Use wisdom.

This can get messy and complex, but when you know what you want, you don't walk around with a chip on your shoulder about not getting it. You're not cocked and ready to fire. You won't ruin the equity you have built and the leadership investment you have made into others. Instead, when you are aware that you are cocked and ready to fire, you can keep yourself from attempting to punish others. You can intentionally downshift to first gear and get what you need internally. Then you will be able to calmly and factually state what has happened and what you need.

It's the same thing at home. It can be as simple as me telling my wife, "It's been a hard day. Can I get a hug?" I'm not making her responsible for the needs of my identity. I'm expressing a desire for comfort. Sometimes it's as simple as making small requests.

You can only ask for what you need if you know what you really need. You don't have to be crushed or experience some kind of manic euphoria if you do or don't get what you need from the others. You stay steady and secure.

Master The Meta-Roles

The third skill to learn is mastering the meta-roles. You know leaders with the philosophy, "That's who I am. If they don't like it they can work somewhere else." That approach is propped up by the claim of living authentically. Yes, it is important to lead from the authentic core of who you are, but let's not confuse roles and identity. Oftentimes what is underneath the steadfast claim of authenticity is a fear of trying other ways of relating. When we feel insecure, we run to what we know, but to master conflict we have to learn to give them what they need. We will learn to fill three meta-roles as the situation needs: empath, leader, and sage.

Empath: The Comforter.

The empath comforts. Your internal security makes you externally attuned. You look for what needs to be comforted and you do it. You speak hope.

Leader: The Director.

The leader directs, decides and empowers. You make the call. But you do it with an eye toward empowering others. You also ask them to make the call. You sacrifice to make the vision a reality.

Sage: The Advisor.

The sage advises. You tell stories and communicate them visually. You invite interest and aren't threatened by protest. You don't lecture. You introspect deeply and give to others from the wisdom you have gained.

Each of these can be falsely judged. The forced empathy is overly syrupy with empty sentimentality. The forced leader is dictatorial. The forced sage speaks nonsense. When these roles are not in a state of proving or hiding they are exactly what the situation needs.

We are typically strong in one, weak in one and mediocre in the other. This isn't about learning your strengths and building your life around those. This is about learning the weak spot in the leadership of your mission and the building of your community. If you can learn to switch roles as the situation demands, then you can bring a dynamic presence to all of your leadership and relationships.

The role I am most comfortable in is leader. If there is chaos around me, I want to power up and take control. If I come home and things feel a little chaotic or I feel falsely threatened in a meeting, my default can be to take over even if I do it under a calm, cool, and collected veneer. Noticing the urge to take over and instead redirecting my energy into the role of empath has significantly improved my ability to relate. I investigate why there is chaos. I validate the fear. Then, the behavior of others can change from an internal relaxed state rather than a forced state that is fear-based. I spent 15 years running hard in the role of leader. Now my work is becoming more about the sage role with some empathy.

It's like a recipe. You don't take out the substance of who you are but you learn to sprinkle in the other roles for flavor. There are so many combinations to experiment with. You will develop your ability to move in and out of these roles as you notice your reactions.

Let's say you get an angry email from a client. Do you need to respond with comfort for their fear as an empath? Do you need to communicate a contractual boundary as the leader? Do you need to build, fix, or communicate a system as the sage? Do you need to do some combination? This isn't being phony. When you know who you are apart from the roles you fulfill, you can move in and out of these as necessary.

Build Healthy Teams

The fourth skill to learn is how to build a healthy team. Part of what you're doing in building relationships is building a team, whether it's your business or family. A common frustration among business leaders is having an employee who isn't a team player. The common approach to solve the problem is to pressure the selfish employee into being more "we focused." You can't have a great "we" unless it's a collection of healthy "me." You can't be a "we" player if you are coming into the team insecure. The person who can't play team ball, who steals credit or who is never wrong isn't that way because she is prideful. It's because she is insecure.

When building a healthy "we" as the team leader, don't worry about smoothing all the rough edges. A common mistake in team leadership is the attempt to make everyone the same because we can't handle the quirky pointedness of people. This happens in family dynamics. We label one child with a certain identity. "You are the funny one." We balk at changing this because together we are whole in the labels we fulfill. The same thing happens at work. We don't allow people to change and try on different identities to grow and expand.

Let people exist in their pointed quirkiness. Let everyone bring the strength, the amplification of who they are, instead of the the dumbed-down, numbed-out version. When they bring that, they can bring their unique contribution. They can bring the beauty of who they are. The team is more whole. The product you create together is better. There will be conflict, but you are learning how to master it.

To be clear, part of learning to master conflict involves understanding there is finesse between letting people make mistakes and rescuing them from self-destruction. When my daughter was learning to ride a bike, I didn't set her course up a hill into oncoming traffic. At the same time, I didn't run beside her at every moment to keep her from skinning her knee.

There are no clear-cut answers. That's why the best leadership comes from secure leaders. They understand there's a lot of discernment involved. As you think about your team and the people you lead, you are looking for ways to set them up for the next win. They may lose and they may skin their knees. In fact, if they're not skinning their knees some, they're not growing at the edge of their abilities.

You can master conflict. It doesn't take a ton of books on communicating better or learning rules so you can posture and ultimately manipulate. It takes learning to order your internal world so you can effectively lead your external world. You don't have to run from the blinking lights and sirens of reactions you fear.

Exercises To Complete:

1. Create a reminder on your phone to reinforce assessing without attacking. For a while my lock screen had two questions: "What are you afraid of?" and "How can I comfort you?" I looked at those as a reminder that I was interacting with human beings. If the people you interact with act insecure or if there is potential for conflict to escalate, think of ways you can comfort their fear. I don't actually ask these questions verbatim. My approach is subtler. But having these questions on my phone was a reminder to think it.

2. Take one situation of conflict and deconstruct it. Think back to a big or reoccurring fight at work or at home. What was going on? How was the anger a signal to the fear? What was the real fear?

3. When you encounter a tense situation today draw on your internal identity space. Internally learn to get what you need when you feel threatened. If you have to leave the room for a minute, then do it. I excuse myself to the bathroom. I go to the bathroom and I organize my thinking. I go to that space in my mind's eye to position myself for an experience of a secure identity. I downshift into first gear. Then I can go back into the situation to give my presence from a secure identity.

4. Ask for what you really need in an interaction with someone. Ask for insight or comfort or reassurance—whatever may be appropriate for the circumstance. You can ask without anxiety when you're learning to live out of internal security.

5. Of the meta-roles, which do you turn to the quickest? Which is the most uncomfortable for you? Try the most uncomfortable role once.

Just because it feels awkward doesn't mean it's a bad decision to relate from that role. Learn over time to mix and match combinations of them as necessary.

6. If you want to further your ability to navigate tough conversations go to: chrismcalister.com/toughconversations

CHAPTER ELEVEN

ENJOY RELATIONSHIPS

Attention is the rarest and purest form of generosity.
SIMONE WEIL

Recently, my daughter wanted some hangout time with me. As a father, one of my greatest joys is when my kids actually want to hang out with me. That night, we decided to go out by ourselves and catch up on what was new in her life over her favorite meal. While driving to the restaurant, I found myself internally distracted by looming tasks from work. Holiday celebrations had already shortened the workweek, new opportunities were quickly approaching, and I was collaborating on a project with a handful of creative people. I felt this tension: I deeply desired to be fully present with my daughter, yet I also wanted to be fully engaged with the work that was in front of me.

Many parents are scared to admit that second tension. They confess the struggle of being fully present in their relationships, but they don't understand why they feel that way. Naming the parallel desire to be fully engaged with work helps us frame our emotions.

It is a good thing to want to be fully engaged with your work. It is also a good thing to desire to be fully present with your family. If you live out of a secure identity, you can learn to do both. Finding security in who you are allows you to enjoy your relationships even during life's struggles.

Three critical actions will help you enjoy your relationships: be present, call yourself out, and find a safe friend.

Be Present

The baseline of enjoying relationships is being present. Being present is being loving. There is no agenda. There is only presence. The best people and the best leaders truly love the people they're leading. When you love others, you will enjoy relationships.

The more you sit with yourself and understand the sacredness of simply being human, the power of your identity and the energy of all of your emotions; the more you can be present with others and recognize their sacredness. This kind of presence will change you and help you learn to feel more secure. You won't feel the need to prove yourself or hide. Great relationships amplify who you are. They don't diminish your being.

The last 10 chapters have been about becoming present with yourself—your pain and fear and joy—with regards to who you are and what you do. Now you can do the same for others. The more you recognize yourself unnecessarily proving or hiding in your own life, the more you will see it in others. The more gracious you are with your own proving and hiding, the more gracious you will be with others.

If you are able to be fully present in that team meeting or in that conversation with a loved one, then you can fine-tune and adjust how you are relating to them so they can see, feel, and hear the gift of you being present with them. You won't connect with them because of what they can give you for your identity. Instead, you can love them how they need to be loved and serve them how they need to be served. Great relationships aren't built on larger-than-life moments. They are built by people who pay attention to small moments and love from a secure identity. Great relationships are not built on dramatic movie moments, but on 10,000 exchanges that communicate, "I see you. I hear you. I feel you." These small moments create and nurture the momentum all great relationships need. The key question to being present is this: Is there any reason I feel afraid, insecure, or hyped that is keeping me from being with this person here and now?

To answer that question, learn to pay attention to what you feel. Maybe in the aftermath of a fight with your spouse you don't feel like walking past him or her and giving a kiss on the cheek. You want to withdraw your love. You want to hide. Pay attention to that tug. Offer your attention in the form of a kiss on the cheek.

Perhaps you think of a person and need to text them or need to walk by their office to check in. Pay attention to that tug. As more time passes before the people you care about hear from you, they will draw a conclusion based on their insecurity. They will fill in blanks with negative reasons as they try to understand why they haven't heard from you. The more you are present with yourself and not distracted by your own insecurity, the more you can be present with others and notice when a period of not sharing a conversation has gone on too long.

Sometimes the needs of others cause us to shy away from giving them what they need. I think of this when I see handicapped parking spaces.

Two thousand years ago the handicapped were shunned and shamed. They were exiled away from others because people assumed there was some evil associated with their ailment. Now, society makes a space for them. Human consciousness still has a long way to go, but we have come so far. Healthy communities and relationships organize around the needs of others. They don't exclude and ignore.

When you are secure in who you are, you give love to people in ways they need to feel loved. You do not love them in a way that suggests you need them to love you back. If your fear is that you are not special or unique and you need validation in those areas, you will want to make people feel as though they are special and unique when you're in a healthy place. We talked about how giving where it hurts shapes your mission. We also reach an elevated level of enjoying relationships when we understand how to love people in the way they need love, not the way we want to express love.

We can organize relationships into three arenas: Teams we lead at work, our friends, and family commitments. We learn what kind of love and attention they need and how to give those in a way that resonates with them. One of my kids might verbally list off all the chores she accomplished. "I put away my laundry, made my bed, and cleaned my room." What is she really saying? "Please celebrate my performance." She needs to know she is loved regardless of her performance. One of my other kids doesn't struggle with believing she is loved; she wants to know that she is safe in my affections. When I am fully present and not blocked up by my own insecurities, I can find creative moments to express that to her.

With our friends, we express love by being aware of their personalities, their natural bents, and their strengths and weakness. Are they introverted? Extroverted? Do they draw energy from being alone or from being around others? We have the ability to notice this when our own fears and insecurity don't block our ability to pay attention. When we grow close to some of those friends, we start to notice their fears. We learn to speak into what they need.

The same idea holds true for people in our work environment. If we are leading a team meeting, evaluating progress or introducing a new initiative, we need to pay attention to the fact that we may have triggered a fear. You know a fear based response has occurred when others power up or hide away. Get to the root of the fear by asking questions.

As you become more present and as you express love, it's important to keep in mind that no matter how secure you are, you will still mess up.

Call Yourself Out To Repair The Tear

My family and I were sitting at the dinner table when my wife said something I disagreed with and felt should have been handled differently. Rather than speaking up about my disagreement, I withdrew in silence but yelled with my face. She called me out on it: "When you disagree with me, you raise your eyebrows." Then my 12-year-old daughter added, "And you let out a breath." They were calling me out on my relational cues. I felt myself become defensive. Everything in me wanted to prove I was right and they were wrong. This is how I operated as a leader and in relationships for more than a decade. Taking that route, I would have gone down in a ball of flames because everyone at the table knew it was true. Instead, I remember feeling this unusual tug to admit I was wrong.

You will be surprised when your internal wiring changes and you realize you feel secure enough to admit you are wrong. Many people believe how you respond to life's circumstances reveals who you are at your core. They say if you shake the cup, what comes out is who you are. The problem with that perspective is it suggests our responses are static and fixed. They are not. We are dynamic. We can change. And the more insights we have about who we are, the more meaningful changes can take place.

When you reframe everything through the filter of identity, every moment has the potential to form who you are. You will either become a better or worse version of yourself. At dinner, in the face of being called out and feeling defensive, I told myself: "Chris, sit here and be wrong, because you are."

This is one of the most painful but important actions you can take in order to better enjoy and appreciate your relationships. Say, "I was wrong." Or maybe you need to say:

"I need help."
"I lied."
"I'm sorry."
"I don't know."

When you are secure, you can be honest about who you are and where you are in your life.

You can't enjoy relationships fully if you have open loops of people you have hurt along the way. As you learn to pay attention to this, you will repair any tears immediately. You may also need to revisit some past situations that created tears in the lives of those around you. There are times I was too aggressive as a leader trying to prove myself and I hurt some people with my decisions. A number of years ago, there were a few people I called and apologized to for poorly executed decisions. To one of them I gave a two-minute prepared speech. When I finished, the line was dead. I thought he had hung up on me. I needed to get my message across so I called back. He said the phone went dead. I repeated my speech and again the same thing happened. I finished the speech and the line was dead. Talk about a humbling, vulnerable experience. I called back a third time. I repeated my speech, again. This time he heard it all. He claimed he had already forgiven me, but I still had to do what was necessary to repair that tear.

If for some reason you can't make that apology—circumstances changed or it feels paralyzing and gut-wrenching—recall the exercise from Chapter 6. Create a space in your mind's eye to play out the experience. What is it like for you to imagine yourself having that conversation with them?

Also, learn to do this activity in the moment. To lead with vulnerability is to call out your own fear in the meeting. Everyone already knows it. You're bringing attention to it in a way that gives them permission to call out their own BS. When you power up and instantly go on the defensive only to become aware of it, have the courage to stop mid-sentence to say, "That came out wrong" or "That might not have come out the way I intended. Let me rephrase that." Or with a renewed sense of identity, you stop throwing out made up answers and say, "I don't know." I don't want to confuse you, though. The point of being a vulnerable leader is not to dump everything on others to make yourself feel better.

A little while ago, one of our kids had an intense coughing sickness. My wife and I were exhausted. We had some conflict with her at bedtime because we wanted her to go to bed earlier since she was sick. She tried to rationalize why. Even though she was sick, tired and had a cough that resembled a barking seal, she didn't think she should have to go to bed before her sisters. Rather than investigating and validating what was happening in that moment, I tried to power up and force the behavior I wanted out of her. It happens at home. It happens as leaders. This is how we mess up. I verbally blew up, and then I felt terrible about it and left the moment. After something like that happens, rather than feeling guilty about your behavior, you will feel shame about who you are. You become blocked up and lose clarity.

I was able to process that and accelerate by downshifting into first gear, identity. After becoming secure in my identity again, I went into her room and apologized and repaired the tear as I overflowed security. She had some insecure reactions to own too, but I let her choose whether or not she wanted to own it. I can't force her to do that, but I decided to own what I had to own. That was my response.

When there are no instances of proving yourself or hiding and you are willing to call yourself out, then conversations with friends exude a level of exhilaration that exceeds calculated performance. You volley vulnerability back and forth. You release control. You engage in the moment, and that moment seems as though it's on fire. But remember, you can't trust everyone at this level.

Safe Friend

To fully enjoy relationships be present and give others the love they need, repair any tears, and finally, find a safe friend. In this safe relationship, there is no proving or hiding, and you can safely call yourself out. By experiencing this safety you reinforce the reality of relaxing your way into who you are. Most people are suffocating in loneliness. They don't know what it's like to have one friend where they don't have to hide or prove themselves in any way.

With my family, I don't have to prove or hide. But I also don't expose them to everything I struggle with because our children are young. That would put too heavy of a burden on them. As they age, I continue to share more without unloading more than they can handle. I try to gently deconstruct any pedestal they would put me on by sharing struggles while also inspiring them by sharing when I win.

I have made some decisions that caused me a tremendous amount of financial fear, but I did not expose my kids to the financial intensity of the moment. I did not hide from them and pretend we were in a better situation than we were. Instead, I shared with them that we are focusing our money in other places.

We have different degrees of relationships. We have a relationship with the public with regards to what we do. We will relate to them in a different way than the inner circle of people we are close to. With our inner circle, we will share a lot more.

There are those one or two people who you don't have to prove anything or hide anything with. They are your safe, redemptive friends. They are safe in that you can tell them something and they won't use it against you or share all your secrets. They are redemptive in that they will help you learn to live out of security. They won't support your self-sabotaging choices, but they won't shame you for making them either.

Any time we talk about safety and vulnerability in relationships, we have to talk about boundaries. If you are in a verbally or physically abusive relationship at work, you need to report that and/or make immediate plans to actively seek new employment. If you have a boss who is manipulative, coercive, overpowering and who is not helping you develop, that situation is different. You may have to play poker in that scenario. Meet that person where they are, be as engaged as they need to see you engaged, and don't let them know you are making a plan to get out of that space.

If you are in a personal relationship that is in any way unsafe, get out. You absolutely need to be safe. When you're secure in who you are, you can establish healthy boundaries. It is a lie that you need that relationship to be whole. Acknowledge this truth and remove yourself if the relationship is unsafe.

The more you are safe with yourself, the more you will attract and develop safe relationships. Safe relationships are the pinnacle of healthy community. You can appreciate them without fixating on them. At the same time, you can avoid the relationship killer when you make yourself responsible for the behavior of another human. Safe people know you're never responsible for another human being's behavior. You can share your fears. You can inspire. You can create environmental conditions that challenge others to grow. But you can never make them grow. When you refuse to carry the responsibility to change another human being, you can be with them for who they are and where they are.

I am constantly meeting leaders who are lonely. I know the price of leadership, and owning a business can definitely take its toll on your friendships. Taking time to invest in the right friendships can be rewarding in all areas of your life. I have a few friends that I can tell anything to. We're building a party with SightShift and we're not trying to force our way into someone else's party.

When you enjoy your relationships, life is fun. You feel good and your leadership becomes infectious. You don't live on a platform or on a stage using false charisma and charm to win people over. People see who you are when they get up close to you. You don't have to share everything in every space, but the more you walk through your vulnerable moments, the more you learn you can share who you are and you're going to be ok. Your relaxed state will attract the most fulfilling relationships. If you remain present and give love, repair tears, and find a safe friend where there are no secrets, your ability to enjoy relationships will flourish. It will add joy to your life and make your leadership more compelling.

Exercise To Complete:

Find one person who you can call yourself out to. Identify a moment you were proving or hiding or when you did something out of insecurity, and call yourself out to that person. Tell them what happened and how you responded. In this place you don't have to have any secrets, and it's amazing. Dealing with relationships in this way is risky and vulnerable, but find a safe friend with whom you don't have to prove yourself or hide. When you're secure in who you are, you can take a risk and not get crushed if it doesn't work out. I know I'm asking you to take a risk. As you take this risk, though, here's a reminder that will allow you to ease your way into it: You're going to be okay.

CHAPTER TWELVE

TEACH WHAT YOU KNOW

Your sacred space is where you can find yourself again and again.

JOSEPH CAMPBELL

Tetherball was my all-time favorite game to play during recess in the sixth grade. Since tetherballs have been banned by most school districts, you may not be familiar with the game. A volleyball is attached by a rope to the top of a tall, metal pole. The goal of the game is to hit the volleyball and be the first person to wrap the rope around the pole. One day, I was about to take my turn when someone else stepped in front of me. I protested, but like a typical bully, the other kid pushed me down. My first response was to hide and do nothing. My second response was to power up and use my lunch money to pay the two biggest guys in our class to be my bodyguards.

So there I was in sixth grade, paying two guys to beat up somebody else for me. The sense of power went to my head. I felt unstoppable. I made fake cigarettes and a cigarette box, and I puffed away next to the fence by the playground. It wasn't long before someone drove by and reported seeing a kid smoking. My teacher figured out it was me, and my operation got shut down.

In seventh grade, I changed schools and had PE for seventh period. Coincidentally, that same bully from the tetherball incident also changed schools and had the same PE class! While we were playing football in class he intentionally pushed me down, causing me to break my wrist. The bully won, twice.

I got bullied and I hid. Then, I powered up and bullied back. It's a vicious cycle. It takes us back to where we began when we understand shame is the internal bully that suffocates your brilliance. Ambitious leaders reveal their insecurity when they hide or try to prove themselves. Unfortunately, they don't understand how to empower others. You, however, have learned throughout this process how to stop shame from being your internal bully. You have learned to empower yourself.

It is my hope that you will maintain your momentum. I want to help sustain your potential for growth, because you have begun a lifetime of exploration. Future experiences and moments of awareness will open up more opportunities to further embrace your identity. Then you can successfully pursue your mission and be present in your relationships free of shame.

You have already done more than most will ever do by noticing your fear and your pain, and by becoming aware. You have been leaning in, bringing important matters to the surface, paying attention, and relaxing into a place of brilliant leadership. You get to choose to become a better or worse version of yourself everyday; to become a more competent leader or an ineffectual one. If you want to continually improve and remain at the edge of your abilities, take this one action:

Teach what you know.

If you can pass on to someone else one idea you have gleamed from this book it will expand itself deeper within you while you empower others. Teaching the content helps you own the content. In order to help you effectively teach what you know, here is a summary of everything you have learned in the previous 11 chapters—an overview of what is the SightShift paradigm.

First, The Three Truths Of SightShift

Truth 1: Shame lies to you about who you are, while fear invites you to accept the lie. These are the fears we talked about in Chapter 2.

Truth 2: Shame blocks the brilliance of your identity. Who you are is a beautiful thing. Shame prevents you from engaging in your mission and the richness of your community by blocking your identity.

Truth 3: Life's moments are an invitation to relax into your brilliance. Shame's power is diminished in those small moments when we lean into the fear and pay attention to it. The more you advance into the fear and pain and reframe everything, the more its power is diminished.

We have to learn to reframe everything, a concept we talked about in Chapter 1. Reframing everything means processing your life according to identity (first gear), mission (second gear), and community (third gear). When you reframe your life, you start by focusing your efforts into first gear. To stay at the edge of your abilities, grow your leadership, feel alive, fight off the paralysis of fear, and resist making others responsible for your identity, you have to constantly reframe everything.

Cooperating with this process of downshifting into first gear and overflowing into your mission so you can be present in your community is wholeness. There is a simple rhythm you can learn that will help you cooperate with the process of identity > mission > community. This visual will teach you how to move through each moment and relax into your brilliance:

The SightShift Paradigm

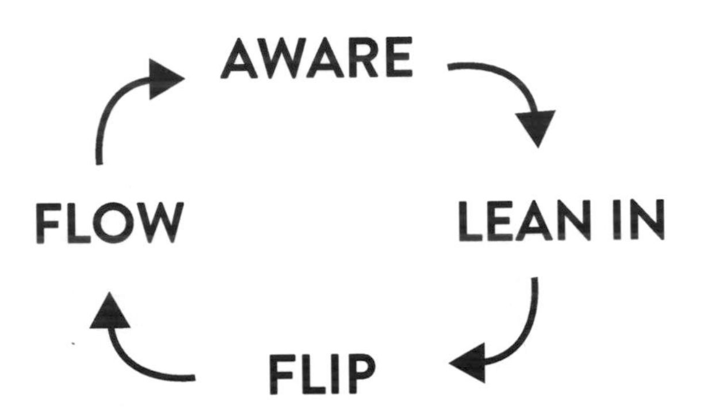

This is the cycle of reframing everything. If you think about this diagram as a compass, the northern aspect is "aware." This book has focused a lot on helping you become aware of the fear. Begin to reframe everything by first reaching north and becoming aware.

The next cardinal direction is east. As you reach east you are leaning into the fear. You're not only aware of it, but you are intentionally leaning towards it. Recall the story in Chapter 3 about the canoeing trip where I had to lean into the rock so the boat wouldn't tip. As you lean into fear and pay attention to those profound micro-moments that happen when you interact with others, you will eventually come around and reach south. South is where you flip the lie. In order to face your fear and turn it around in the moment, you must learn to enter that space you built in your mind's eye even if you need to excuse yourself from the situation. In this place, you can use that connection to trigger yourself and flip the lie. Proclaim to yourself, "Right now I feel threatened, I feel afraid, and all of that is a false threat to my identity because no one defines me, and no mission defines me." Realize the opposite of the lie and receive abundance in those moments.

After flipping the lie you're able to reach west and flow. You rest because you are secure. There's no proving or hiding. You are. You serve, perform, relate, and live from abundance. You give from the wholeness within you. It's like the four seasons. In the fall, we are aware. We let go of our attachment to insecurity and lean into the pain by embracing winter. In the winter, it might seem that nothing is happening, but our core is gaining strength. We survive the letting go and the pain to find new life in the spring. We flip the lie in spring when we find empowerment in who we are regardless of the state of our circumstances or relationships. As new life blossoms, we enter the flow of summer. We rest. We give to others from our overflow.

Life isn't static. We don't reach a state of perfect internal security. Life is dynamic. Abundance and scarcity are an infinite loop. We experience abundance, which scarcity then threatens. We feel secure and then we feel afraid. What do you do when you feel afraid? Go back to becoming aware, reach east to lean in, reach south and flip the lie, and finally reach west and hit flow.

As you are secure in who you are, abundance overflows, leading you to a clearly defined mission, and you are able to build a healthy community. It's a process of reframing everything. Allow the SightShift Compass of becoming aware, leaning in, flipping the lie, and utilizing flow to guide you daily. You might have multiple moments in a day where you are downshifting or accelerating to better process your life with regards to identity. This paradigm can be as macro or micro as you need it be. You may be able to pass through all four seasons within a few minutes while other areas of your life may feel like you are stuck in a single season for years. You have permission to be where you are.

Don't aim to a certain standard of peace. Life will never be as stress-free externally as you want it to be. Aim to quickly recognize when you have lost center and step back into awareness.

You can't jump from fall to summer no matter how much self-help hype tries to convince you otherwise. You can't move backwards into rest. The place you want to run from is the place you're being invited to because it is the place you can discover your brilliance. You can't analyze your way into flow. You can't force your way into flow. You notice and you accept reality. You downshift. You position yourself for change using the identity space and identity activity. You grow. You overflow. You are present.

All the strategies in this book are intentional so you can learn to position yourself to live and love with a secure identity. But there is one catch: You don't know it all and neither do I.

I still fall into fear and I still struggle. The one secret that keeps me learning and living out the practices I have been sharing is teaching what I know. You will stay sharpest not only by living out this way of life, but also by talking about it. As your brain organizes itself around these practices and you start to describe them to others, they become even more profound. Find a person and tell them something you learned about identity, mission, and community. It might be that safe friend. It might flow out of an unplanned conversation at work. The more you talk about it, the more it will permeate your thinking.

Here's my challenge for you: Share the identity, mission, or community paradigm with one person. Put it in your own words. Do it however you want, but do it. You will be doing them a favor because they will learn how to order their internal world, and that generosity is going to come back to you in some way. Become an empowering leader and teach what you know.

Exercise To Complete:

Life moves fast, and we can start mindlessly forgetting what it means to reframe everything. We get ahead of ourselves and we leave our internal worlds behind. We need the big picture view for our lives and the small moments that make them up.

Think about how the identity > mission > community paradigm, and the practice of reframing everything has helped you. What does it mean for you to become aware, lean in, flip the lie, and flow? How can you share the benefits of this practice with someone else? A lifetime of exploration has begun.

When I launched full time into this work and received my first call for a large corporate gig, I bragged to my wife, "It's happening!" My first conversation with the corporation revealed they had made some new hires, there were a couple of demotions, and several new initiatives did not have buy-in from the team. The human resource liaison asked if I could come in and lead some fun events for the day, including trust falls, to help the team bond. I didn't mean to, but I laughed out loud. The troubles this company was experiencing couldn't be resolved with something as simple as a trust fall exercise. I said, "Here's what I would want to do. Let me come in and speak about how fear blocks us up. I'll tell stories. We'll laugh. Everyone will learn how to lead secure and relax their way into their brilliance. I'll guide them through exercises that will help them learn how to continue reframing everything. The team members will be able to articulate what blocks them from fully engaging. We'll unleash their ambition and develop practices to help them relate. If I come in and do trust falls, everything will immediately go back to the same dysfunction once the false, hyped-up veneer fades." She said, "I don't know if we would want that." I said, "Well then, I'm not your guy."

Do you want a flash of hyped up self-help to gloss over the dysfunction that might be driving your team and your relationships or are you ready to build a strong foundation? When you become secure in your identity, you develop the ability to lead healthy, productive teams and take more ground in your industry. If you are ready to build something of significance, well then, I'm your guy.

Work with Chris:
https://www.chrismcalister.com/work-with-chris/

ENDNOTES

Chapter 2

*I am attempting to rework contributions from fields of personality development and typology. This book sparked my thinking years ago: Riso, Don Richard and Russ Hudson. 1999. The wisdom of the enneagram. New York City: Bantam.

Chapter 5

*I'm reworking some categories from a study that was done in the 1950's called The Lonely Crowd that found as societies progress, they can shift from being driven by tradition, to finding their own internal voice, learning their own self and being guided by that, and then directed by others.

Chapter 6

* http://jn.physiology.org/content/112/12/3219
audio link in exercise:
http://chrismcalister.podbean.com/e/no-more-proving-or-hiding/

Chapter 10

chrismcalister.com/toughconversations

What if we could learn the essentials for building a life we love?

We could focus on what matters.

You can learn the 7 mistakes that will build a life you hate.

TheRiderbook.com

Made in the USA
Charleston, SC
11 January 2016